Still Teaching in the
Key of Life

Joyful Stories From
Early Childhood Settings

Mimi Brodsky Chenfeld

National Association for the Education
of Young Children
1313 L Street NW, Suite 500
Washington, DC 20005-4101
202-232-8777 • 800-424-2460
www.naeyc.org

NAEYC Books

Chief Publishing Officer
Derry Koralek

Editor-in-Chief
Kathy Charner

Director of Creative Services
Edwin C. Malstrom

Managing Editor
Mary Jaffe

Senior Editor
Holly Bohart

Senior Graphic Designer
Malini Dominey

Associate Editor
Elizabeth Wegner

Editorial Assistant
Ryan Smith

Through its publications program, the National Association for the Education of Young Children (NAEYC) provides a forum for discussion of major issues and ideas in the early childhood field, with the hope of provoking thought and promoting professional growth. The views expressed or implied in this book are not necessarily those of the Association or its members.

Back cover photograph: Taryn Terwilliger

Cover design: Eddie Malstrom

Illustrations and drawings are courtesy of the author

A copublication of the National Association for the Education of Young Children and Redleaf Press, 10 Yorkton Court, St. Paul, MN 55117.

Library of Congress Control Number: 2013951456

ISBN: 978-1-938113-01-7

NAEYC Item 173

To my mighty seven grandchildren: Len, Callie, Dylan, Chloe, Ryan, Noah, and Landen

To my fabulous children: Cliff and Chana, Cara and Jim, Dan and Kristi

To the memory of my anchor man, Howard, and to the memory of my parents, Iris and Joe, and my parents in love, Rose and Charlie Chenfeld

To ALL of our children and the very special people who answer the call to love, care for, and teach them

The following stories were published previously in *Teaching in the Key of Life:*

There's a Wolf at Your Door
"My Loose is Tooth!" Kidding Around With the Kids
Hangin' Out With the Muffin Man
We Drew a Circle That Took Him In

The following stories were previously published in *Teaching by Heart:*

"Do Spiderwebs Ever Wake You Up?"
On Wednesdays I Can't
As We Believe, So We Teach
No Rx for Reading
Get the Elephant Out of the Room!
Once Upon a Time: The End!
A Letter to the Families and Friends of the Children in Room 13

The following stories were previously published in *Celebrating Young Children and Their Teachers:*

My Next Fifty Years
My Puppet Is on Ritalin
Education Is a Moving Experience
Uh-Uh! None of This "I'm Not Creative" Stuff!
Why I'm Still Hanging Out With the Kids

The following stories appeared in *Young Children* or *Teaching Young Children:*

It's Hard to Smile With a Binky in Your Mouth
The Elf and the Butterfly

Contents

Foreword

The book you are about to read is not prescriptive. There's no specific practice to be mastered in a programmatic manner or in a given sequence. For Mimi Brodsky Chenfeld, teaching must be the opposite: an exuberant, improvisational, always-tuned-into-the-moment experience with individual children whose capacity and keenness for learning cries out like a survival instinct. (It is one, after all.) The only method and strategy that Mimi would have you follow is to follow your heart.

This book you are about to read is nothing new. Mimi would be the first to say that she wishes only to tell you what you know, what you've sensed all along, but, perhaps, have not yet honored. (That said, her nearly 60 years of teaching surely have a lot to tell.)

Imagine, if you will, three kinds of teachers.

The first stands at a blackboard. It's covered with photographs and charts and cartoon characters holding vocabulary words. This teacher's lesson sounds like this: *Here is the subject we need to learn. Does everyone see it? Very good.* The "blackboard" teacher is the "view" . . . and it becomes the students' "view."

The second teacher stands beside a window. Its frame holds the view, and all the students have a look for themselves. The "window" teacher sounds like this: *Do you see what I see? Does anyone see anything else? Very good.*

The third teacher stands a giant mirror against the classroom wall and then sits among the children and the windows and the view outside that's reflected in the glass. There is no description of what the students should see. No questions. And such teaching sounds like this: [silence].

It's the sound of listening. That "reflective" teacher is providing a chance for every child to hear themselves think, to see for themselves, to let their senses fill, and to open their imaginations. *Very good.*

At certain moments, we may all feel more comfortable teaching as a blackboard. We may need to teach as a window, gathering eager young faces at a window to spy something of this old world with their new eyes. But I believe the book you are about to read will embolden you to honor that reflective teacher you can be. A teacher whose passion and confidence can spontaneously recognize content in unprepared moments and unexpected places. A teacher who can create an atmosphere where serious inquiry partners with contagious laughter, and each child's unique curiosities, abilities, and "views," are all celebrated within a caring, respectful community of fellow learners.

If the Art of Teaching had a muse, her name would be Mimi. Let the pages here inspire you just as each day you, her fellow teacher, set forth to inspire your own eager learners.

—Michael J. Rosen,
Creative educator and author of more than
a hundred books for children and adults

November 2013

Still Teaching in the Key of Life

Whatever else good teaching is, it is teaching in which our hearts and minds are fully engaged in connecting with children's hearts and minds. This is what I call "teaching in the key of life."

I met a teacher I hadn't seen for many years. He asked if I was still teaching. "Of course," I answered. His eyes showed his surprise. "I'm going to keep trying until I get it right," I said.

The stories in this book are notes from that journey— the journey *all* educators take as we bump along, losing and then finding our way again, stopping at scenic over- looks, detouring at danger spots, speeding along on cruise control, crawling through traffic snarls.

I started teaching young children on a stage in the gym of an overcrowded school in upstate New York in 1956. The United States had a teacher shortage then. We had few materials—no high-interest, low-vocabulary, brand-new books; no overhead projectors, video libraries, or computers. Just the children and us!

Since that time I've worked with all types of individuals and in all kinds of situations—from toddlers to senior citizens, from the gifted and talented to those with learning disabilities and other special needs, from Head Start programs to Upward Bound, from the inner city to the suburbs, from New York to Hawaii. The things that I believed then, I believe now—only more strongly. My beliefs started out flimsy, easy to blow over, almost as fragile as the House Made of Straw. Time, and the children I have worked with, helped me to turn the straw into bricks. I believe in loving children, in loving people. I believe in caring, playfulness, sharing, and courage. Today, these beliefs are as solid as the House Made of Bricks. No wolf or wind can blow *this* house over.

I once was driving to a conference in Canfield, Ohio. The directions Muriel Hampton had given me were excellent, and I followed them to the letter—and got totally, dismally lost. I ended up outside of a restaurant and called Muriel.

"This is where I am," I said. "I don't know where it is. Please, come and meet me!"

Muriel was astonished. "You're only a mile away. But it's impossible for you to be at that restaurant if you followed my directions!"

We in education know that the impossible is our everyday reality. Sometimes, the prescribed way to reach our destination is not the way that succeeds. We have our educational goals, our directives, our curriculum guidelines. Often, we are given preset ways to accomplish those goals. Sometimes those ways don't work. Now, if those goals, approaches, and curricula are attuned to children's ages, stages, interests, and feelings, they are more likely to work. Even so, we mustn't think there is only one approach to helping children learn. There are many ways to reach our destination. A Native American saying goes something like this: "Let all the paths recognize each other."

When I worked with children in an urban school through their Artists-in-the-Schools program, I walked into one of the rooms while the children were at recess. This gave me a few minutes to explore before they came back. The walls of this room were papered with rules: If you do this, that will happen to you; if you dare to do this twice, these things will be your punishment; and so on. Each item was very specific—sit in this position, line up in that location. The rules covered every moment, every behavior possibility.

After reading these rules, I expected the world's most obedient, cooperative, and courteous children to enter the room. Instead, I was almost trampled by rude, rough, mean-spirited children running, fighting, and shouting their way in. This group was one of the most difficult I have worked with. I was dismayed by their behavior.

After our session, I had a chance to spend a few minutes with their frustrated teacher, who told me, "These are the toughest children I have taught in 10 years of teaching." I looked at her room of ignored rules and collective rudeness and responded honestly, "If something isn't working, don't keep doing it."

We talked for a while. I shared my feelings. "These rules aren't working with these children. Every class is a special mix of specific individuals. Every year is a new year. Maybe nothing you have ever studied will work with this particular group of children. You'll have to try everything—known and unknown, old and new—to find a way to reach them. What do they care about? What do they respond to? What touches them? What are their interests? When are they most responsive? Who are their heroes?"

As I left that classroom, a child slipped me a note. It read, "Please don't leave us."

I want to launch a nationwide anti-smug campaign. I am meeting more and more children who already know everything!

"We already studied colors!"

"We already had the human body in second grade!"

"We did nutrition last year!" (I told the children who uttered this protestation about the scientist Barbara McClintock, who studied kernels of corn on the cob for more than 60 years and still felt she hadn't learned everything there was to know about corn.)

Educators and parents, join the anti-smug campaign! Down with the convergent thinking and closed, absolute, right or wrong answers. Up with divergent thinking and open-ended exploring, brainstorming, wonder-full discussions and questions!

I believe—have always believed—that there are no unreachable children, only those who are, as yet, unreached. That is a leap of faith. As we believe, so we teach. I think this Edwin Markham poem is the core of what education is all about:

He drew a circle that shut me out—
Heretic, rebel, a thing to flout.
But love and I had the wit to win:
We drew a circle that took him in.

The great teachers I know are circle drawers. They never accept being left out or leaving a child out. They continually make larger and larger circles to take in an alienated child, to turn a child from *off* to *on*, to help a child who knows only failure to taste success, to change the history of a child with a broken self-image. Never give up on a child! Sometimes you may be the only person who hasn't given up—even with a very young child. Sometimes you are the only person drawing that circle, the only person believing in that child.

Think about the Yiddish proverb "All of my children are prodigies." If you believe this and live it every day, you'll find that it's true. I have never had a child who did not demonstrate originality, creativity, imagination, surprising talents. The children are all there waiting for us to believe in them, to expect the best from them. In this high-tech, high-anxiety, computer-crazed, supercharged age, children need us to hallow them more than ever. Through it all, do you have the courage?

I once conducted a workshop with education majors who were sharing projects from their teaching practicums. One team reported on an outstanding zoo project that had involved the student teachers and children in weeks of writing, reading, researching, math, art, and science—all the curriculum strands interwoven (as occurs in all good education). One of the subtopics was a listing of endangered species that the 8-year-old children had researched. The student teachers read the list. I felt my hand raise and heard myself say, "There's an endangered species you forgot—*the spirits of children.*"

I'm worried about our children. In our pressured, hurry-up educational system, many of them are learning earlier than ever to be failures, to lose faith in themselves, to feel inhibited, squelched, defeated, discouraged, closed off, anxious, apathetic.

Frayda Turkel and Miriam Flock Schulman, teachers who taught in an Artists-in-the-Schools program, shared music and dance with children who had physical challenges. In keeping with the school's inclusive goals, a class of children without disabilities also came to the program with their teacher, who turned out to be an uptight, stern, joyless person. The dance teachers drummed, chanted, talked, and sang. Children in wheelchairs, with walkers, in braces eagerly participated. Only the children with no disabilities sat, never moving, frozen in their seats by their teacher's stern stare. Which children had the real limitations?

The director of a preschool and her staff took a day off to visit another program in the city. They observed young children learning in silence with minimal interaction with each other, passive lessons, formal instruction, and endless rounds of worksheets. When the children went to the restroom, they walked in single file with their hands on top of their heads. Talking wasn't allowed.

That night the director watched a television program about prisoners of war. She gasped as she watched the prisoners walk in single file, hands on top of their heads. Talking wasn't allowed.

Today, we still have classrooms of harsh silence and of fear. The spirits of our children are endangered. Let's preserve the minds and spirits of our children and ourselves as fiercely as we fight to preserve endangered species like seals and whales.

In my teaching journey, I've come more and more to the conclusion that there are only two choices in education:

Life and Death. If your teaching is indifferent, neutral, apathetic, you are on the side of Death—Death of ideas, of excitement, of discovery. Death of the spirit.

If you are on the side of Life, you can't go wrong. Oh, you can make mistakes, lose your way, misunderstand your goals, and misinterpret directions, but you can't go wrong with children who know you love them and are committed to their welfare, to their minds, to their healthy growth—dedicated to the sacredness of your precious time together.

Rhoda Linder took her preschoolers on a field trip and got lost. They wandered around for a while, with Rhoda becoming increasingly flustered and embarrassed. When they finally reached their destination, 4-year-old Peter beamed his shining smile up at her and burst out, "We're very proud of you."

Stop on the journey with me and spend a little time with teachers who are on the side of Life, teachers like...

... Ronni Hockman Spratt, a teacher of children with special needs and a shouter, screamer, laugher, hugger, lover, friend, taskmaster. No doubt about where she stood on Life or Death: She voted life all the way! She told children who had had numerous experiences with failure, "You are not going to fail in my class. Even if you try, I won't let you! Do you hear me? I won't permit it! You are going to succeed (or else)." She cajoled, threatened, rewarded, joked, tickled, celebrated. Her children succeeded. All education should be special!

... Dawn Heyman, another teacher who has a love affair with teaching and the children in her class. They come from the inner city, from single-parent homes, from families whose home language is a language other than English. Even when they're sick, the children in her class come to school. They don't want to miss a minute.

One of Dawn's students asked her, "Do you know what my four favorite things in the world are?" Dawn couldn't guess.

"Number one is school. Number two is school. Number three is school. Number four is school."

. . . And Mary Sue Garlinger, a movement educator who visited a class for the day and later received a letter from one of the children. "Thank you for coming today," it said. "You made me happy for the rest of my life."

There are so many life-filled teachers, principals and directors, parents, and children on the journey—walking with us, lighting our way, enriching the trip—that I could fill a book with their names alone. I am lucky to know them and feel their warmth. In our field of education, sometimes our lights dim and get buried beneath a bombardment of instructional strategies, methods, and materials. In spite of the pressures, we need to dig out our courage to teach in ways that are loyal to the spirits of young children. I agree with the Tin Woodman, who said, "Brains are not the best thing in the world. . . . Once I had brains, and a heart also; so, having tried them both, I should much rather have a heart."

The stories in this book are notes from the heart.

The First (Almost) 60 Years Are the Hardest!

Good teaching must always be seen as work in progress. Those who share the journey of educating children will find in these observations much to amuse, encourage, and inspire.

The summer I was 16, I worked as a sales clerk at Loft's Candy Store. I was fired because I couldn't wrap. (These days I'm better at *rapping!*) Those two weeks were the only ones in my entire work life that I wasn't with children or involved in issues that concerned children. (Imagine if I *had* been able to wrap!)

The following summer, my friend Rhoda and I were counselors at a sleep-away camp, Jekoce, an hour out of New York City. We had the "baby bunk": Our campers were the infants and toddlers of senior counselors and other camp staff. I've always loved babies, but the summer I spent hanging out with those smart, honest, creative, hilarious little ones started me on a lifelong love affair with our youngest learners. Today, with all-day, five-day-a-week programs for these tiniest humans, I'm still filled with awe, delight, respect, and feelings of responsibility to preserve their sacred spirits.

My first year of teaching, on a stage in an old, worn, country school—with no walls, thick theatrical curtains, weird lights, and no specialists or lunch breaks or bathroom breaks for teachers—I was the young, off-the-wall teacher on a staff of strict, linear-thinking, veteran teachers. Their welcome to me was, let's say, tepid. That trial-by-fire year I learned many lessons. The most important lesson: *I had to be myself.* No matter the pressures pushing conformity, inhibiting spirit, or squelching creativity, I had to be true to what I believed was right for the children. Long before Howard Gardner's multiple intelligences theory emerged, I energized my basic texts with dance, laughter, improvisation, and hands-on activities.

A few years ago I heard from a man who was once a boy in that fourth grade so long ago. Now a grandfather, he had come across one of my books and tracked me down. We talked for an hour. He remembered things I had totally forgotten. What hit me most about that special conversation was his saying, "Mimi, do you know what I remember most clearly from that year? You read us stories from *Winnie-the-Pooh* and we danced!"

When people ask me how long I've been teaching movement, dance, and rhythms to young children, I tell them, "I have never taught one child how to move or dance. My claim to fame is moving, dancing, laughing, and celebrating *with* them. They already know!"

That first year in my class I also had a little girl, Agnes, who was sad and quiet and could easily get lost in the busyness of the day. One early autumn afternoon we were all out in the field playing ball. I was pitching. I noticed Agnes sitting under a tree, her head down, her shoulders slumped. I yelled, "Time out!" and ran over to her. She was crying as if her heart would break. *What's the matter?* I thought.

Right under my nose, Agnes had been left out of games and friendships by cliques that had formed in the class. How could I have missed such an unacceptable situation? I was upset at myself for not seeing what was now obvious, furious at the children for alienating one of their class-mates, and devastated at Agnes's loneliness and feelings of rejection. I stopped the game, called the other children over, and told them to look at Agnes and tell me why she was crying. I couldn't go on with our game or with class-work until this was resolved, so we sat under the tree for the rest of the afternoon. We talked, we all cried, and when it was over, we made promises never to let a child be hurt in our "family."

I knew then and I know now how easy it is for children to gang up, bully others, form tightly knit cliques, and leave others out, and I know too well how easy it is for teachers to miss such goings-on. I urge every adult in any relationship with children to treat these tragic situations as *emergency* scenarios that must be attended to immediately. When one child suffers from bullying, when one child is left out or put down, *everyone* is hurt and the spirit of the group is destroyed. The safety net is torn, and we all fall through.

After the Agnes crisis and resolution we became a hugging, affectionate, loving family group. During recess, welcomes, and farewells, even the boys got hugs from me. We had so much fun! Many of the children hated weekends and pretended to be healthy when they were sick so they wouldn't miss school. I wore a black-and-white tweed winter coat that year, with a fake white fur collar that draped around the shoulders. During winter break I took my coat to the dry cleaner. I hadn't noticed that the white on the fake fur collar was now a strange grayish color. The clerk asked, "What happened to your coat?"

There was only one explanation: months' worth of small faces rubbing against the collar as we hugged during our morning hellos, recess, and afternoon goodbyes. The dry cleaner concluded that the collar was so discolored it could not be cleaned. He recommended it be cut off and a narrower throat collar redesigned and sewn. And it was. But I can still see that coat collar with the stamp of the children's faces deep in its fake fur.

The poet Theodore Roethke reminds us that teaching is "one of the few professions that permits love." For more than 50 years I have suggested to education students and inservice teachers, "If you don't *love* children, do, for their sake and yours, consider a career change!" I wish I had kept that collar.

My husband's favorite hobby is magic. One day when I attended a magicians' convention with him, I couldn't help thinking of my talented, dedicated colleagues. I thought of the magic in *their* hands, the amazing, mind-boggling, heartstring-plucking tricks of the trade that they performed every day, to rare applause:

- Welcoming children who know little or no English and helping them learn their new language while also supporting their home language
- Reassuring crying, clinging toddlers that they are in a safe place
- Comforting children afraid to try, so that they may find the courage to do so
- Guiding children who never play with others to reach out and touch another hand

I am proud to call these magic makers my friends and colleagues.

Michelangelo's motto, "I am still learning," is so on target. No matter what our subject areas, grade levels, or students' ages, we learn every day as we teach. Over the years I've spent treasured times with children from infancy to adolescence, from children trying to go about their lives while staying in homeless shelters to children who go home to loving families in nice houses. With *all* those students, I have found ways to play with ideas that delight and intrigue me.

Many of those ideas—the best ones—come from the children. And wherever it comes from, an idea is a good idea if *you* like it. If you don't like it, you probably shouldn't try it—unless, of course, it's a required part of your program's curriculum. The challenge in that case is to find imaginative ways to enrich that idea. An idea has its own life, and the fun of creative teaching is messing around with ideas until they take flight. Unfortunately, this stressed-out, tested-out time we live in leaves some teachers and children little opportunity to celebrate and explore all the dimensions of their original ideas in order to fully experience the joy of learning. Our courageous, imaginative, confident, fiercely independent, knowledge-able, and gifted teachers can take heart from their sisters and brothers who kept learning alive during the darkest times in history—slavery, war, the Holocaust, famine, and natural disaster, to name a few tragic chapters in the human story.

Too many excellent teachers at all levels are leaving education. This difficult time for our very special family—those who are called to this field because they want to be with children in healthy, helpful, connecting, and inspiring ways—has been painfully challenging. Sadly, when teachers look around and see what appears to be a growing number of decision makers in our society who do not honor research findings, who do not honor principles of developmentally appropriate practices, many head for the exit sign. But teachers who stay, who keep the faith, who keep the children at the center of their focus, are like the heroes and heroines of history who walked along with the children, even through the thickest darkness.

My journey into the next 50 years has already begun. In my backpack for the adventure I carry my puppet, Snowball, my tambourine, all my songs, a purple scarf to remind me of our magic, and the clear memory of a much-hugged fake fur collar on a black-and-white tweed coat. When I think of the collar, I remember that love and kindness must be the air that sweetens our learning.

I should have kept that collar!

There's a Wolf at Your Door

When teachers feel pressured to conform to teaching practices or agendas different from the ones they believe are good for children, they may need to become bilingual—to speak the educational lingo of the day when necessary, while continuing to speak the language of the spirit in their own classrooms.

Feeling stressed, overwhelmed, intimidated? Finding yourself inarticulate, defensive, insecure? Pulled and pushed by the pressures of persistent criticism, accusations, inappropriate demands? Is your flame blowing out?

I'm here to help.

First, build a house of beliefs and commitments. Don't construct your house out of sticks and straw. Too flimsy! Any wolf can blow it over. Your house of beliefs and commitments must be made out of bricks—a strong, sturdy structure resistant to quaking events, unexpected knocks on the door.

Then, on every windowsill of your house, place a sign facing inward. The sign states, *Bilingual Classroom: Two Languages Spoken Here.*

If your house of beliefs is made of bricks, you are fluent in two basic languages. The first is the language of spirit. It includes the vocabulary of adventure, excitement, serendipity, delight, surprise, amazement, imagination, curiosity, experimentation, integration, playfulness, and humor. It is the language of the heart, the language of the ear *inside* the heart. And deep within, if you listen, you can hear the arts. This is the sacred language of learning in an environment aglow with warmth, love, respect, trust, mutuality, encouragement. In this language the first syllable of *fundamentals* is celebrated—fun! All who come to be with you share the motto the children and teachers in the Reggio Emilia, Italy, programs live: Nothing Without Joy. This language speaks the spirit of the wonder of learning. It lights the way for you and all of the children (all of your prodigies) as you share a special time, which will never come again.

But the wolf at the door is not interested in the spirit language, which is why you must be bilingual. What kind of language will keep wolves from huffing and puffing and blowing down your house of beliefs? Wolves at the door demand to know that you know what you are doing at all times. They challenge you to be accountable, clear, concise, knowledgeable, and responsible. They want to know that you are thoroughly conversant in the latest terminology of institutionalized education. In this language, words like *standards, methodology, outcomes, goals and objectives, skills, time on task, assessment, standardized testing,* and *classroom management* are high on the vocabulary list. (Learn them, the wolves say. Know them. Write them 50 times in your workbook. Use them in sentences.)

Who are the wolves at the door? The wolf may be a colleague—"Don't you think your class needs more . . . seatwork? Want to borrow any worksheets?"

The wolf may be a parent—"Other teachers have reading groups. Why don't you?"

The wolf may be a child—a cool, know-it-all child—who says, "I've already seen that on video. That's not the way to tell that story!"

The wolf may be an administrator—"Just exactly what is going on in this classroom? The music is so loud, and all that laughter—where is the teacher?"

The wolf could be a community representative—"Clearly it's because of teachers like you—frills teachers—that the school levy failed! We'll never catch up with other countries' scores with such frivolity. Creativity is definitely out of the curriculum in this district. Back to the basics!"

Or the wolf might be . . . *can* it be? . . . oh, no . . . the worst wolf of all: yourself. "I couldn't possibly let a puppet give my spelling test. What a stupid idea. And frankly, I just don't have the nerve to let the children use playdough to form their spelling words. I'd be a laughingstock."

You may be a bit confused and wondering, "Just how can I use this bilingual concept in my everyday life?" Let me give you a few examples.

Example 1

About to begin my Artist-in-the-Schools residency, I asked the kindergarten teacher what she was doing with the class that was special. She answered, "The short vowel sound of *e*" (eh).

Thinking she was kidding, I joked, "Wow! Isn't that special?" But she was serious. Because I had brought my tambourine, music, and puppets, her kindergartners were eagerly awaiting the promise of something exciting.

So, we celebrated the color red. We turned ourselves into red elves. We made up a yell for red elves. (In the yell, we added the wonderful word *yes*.) On the shelves were shells. We held them to our ears. We did red elf exercises.

When we heard a knock on the door and a concerned wolf asking, "For heaven's sake, what's going on here?," I didn't mumble in tongue-tied incoherence. After all, I'm bilingual!

Using the spirit language, I explained, "Through songs, dances, cheers, poems, exercise, and shells on the shelves, we're delightfully discovering an important sound!"

My friend standing in the doorway look puzzled. "Huh?"

Immediately and authoritatively, I replied, "We are learning the short vowel sound of *e*."

"Oh. Sorry to disturb you," apologized the wolf, and she closed the door gently as she left.

"My Loose Is Tooth!"
Kidding Around With the Kids

Sharing humor and playfulness with children works many wonders. It breaks open and rearranges closed-in ways of thinking, relieves tension and anxiety, and multiplies the fun of learning.

The old folktale goes something like this: At the beginning of time, the Creator was giving out special gifts to each animal. After all the animals received their gifts, the Creator realized that he had forgotten to give something to human beings. To make up for this oversight, he gave them the best gift of all—a sense of humor!

Meet Steve Wilson, a clinical and consulting psychologist who calls himself the One-and-Only-Joyologist. His favorite motto is "If It's Not Fun, I Don't Want To Do It."

Steve spouts statistics and research that overwhelmingly support the importance of humor and playfulness in the classroom. He tells us that teachers who encourage laughter in their classes have children who learn quickly, retain more, and have fewer classroom problems. He urges us to see true, healthful humor as a cathartic activity and a way of relaxing, communicating, sharing experiences, keeping brain cells open and charged, learning, comprehending, developing language, and even clarifying values.

Well, we work with young children! We *know* how easily and enthusiastically they laugh. Their mirth is natural. If they don't understand something meant to be funny, they don't force laughs to be polite as adults often do. We really don't need Steve's research reports to demonstrate that children's laughter indicates comprehension, imagination, and perception. Because language is still new to them, young children are constantly experimenting with words and sounds and phrases, often coming up with original discoveries that astonish and delight. Most young children have amazing memories and are very loyal to sequential events. Give them time and opportunities to share the way they see things. Not only will you learn a lot about the levels of knowledge unique to each child, but you will also have many opportunities to laugh together.

Often, children's explanations of everyday phenomena are highly original. They help us see connections and relationships that are surprising and refreshing and have their own inner logic. The laughter that results is often the laughter of surprise and discovery.

We were talking about whistling. Six-year-old Alicia whispered to me, "Mimi, I'm a very good whistler."

I murmured a response.

"Do you know why I'm such a good whistler?" she asked.

"Why?"

"Because I have a bird."

The more I thought about that explanation, the more it soared in my mind. Of course, the hugs and loving laughter that followed warmed both of us. Laughter is never to make fun of others. To delight with and share and celebrate together, yes. To ridicule, no. That difference makes *all* the difference.

Because young children have not solidified stereotyped attitudes, their reactions to questions and situations are honest—often expressing powerful insights in sometimes hilarious terminology. Asked how she liked her 1-year-old brother, Max, 7-year-old Saroj thought for a moment and then answered, "Forty percent."

Young children have a logic that is unique and pure. For example, a group of kindergartners and I were gathering suggestions on various means of transportation as material for a dance. During a pause in these efforts, I asked "Does anyone have any more ideas on different kinds of transportation?"

Peter immediately contributed, "Yes, Dad's shoulders!" In countless, delightful ways, young children remind us of things we have forgotten. They keep telling us never to take anything for granted. They continually make connections.

Another time, we were improvising a story with many animals in it. During a rest break I asked the children to think of any animals that we might have left out of the story. Four-year-old Timmy immediately noted that "We left out chickmunks!" *Chipmunks* has never sounded right to me since.

I could go on sharing examples of everyday humor in the classroom that help us remember the delightful surprises in store for those of us who celebrate *mirth*days. Children's natural humor—based on their interpretations of language, their honest reactions to situations and relationships, their comprehension of ideas, and their original expressions of wonder and curiosity—provides daily nourishment of laughter, playfulness, and imagination.

Very little is asked of the adults in the children's lives except to provide numerous opportunities for language interaction and free play and to have the good sense to appreciate the children's contributions. But here's the real challenge: We must become more active participants in the humor process. We must free ourselves so we can enjoy a new way (or is it an old way?) of being with our students. Experimental, lighthearted, fun loving, and reassuring, we can be role models, inspirations to our children as we demonstrate through our behavior and our own freedom of speech how to minimize tensions with a joke, how to loosen uptight and closed-in thinking systems—with good-natured kidding, redirecting, and challenging—as we help children deepen their comprehension, build confidence, and enjoy the learning process.

When we take a more active part in the process, we give ourselves permission to goof around. Try "forgetting" facts and have the children catch you. Mixing up information that they know is guaranteed to foster good-humored fun and high-powered clarification and comprehension.

I always kid the children in some of these ways:

"Let's see, folks, today we're going to review one of our very favorite stories: *Goldilocks and the Seven Pigs.*"

Here are listening skills at work. "WHAT? YOU MEAN *GOLDILOCKS AND THE THREE BEARS!*" the children shout.

I interrupt their protests with a twinkly-eyed apology, "Sorry about that, friends. What I mean, let's see, today we're going to review one of our very favorite stories: *Goldilocks and the Three Blind Billy Goats!*"

The variations on this theme are numerous. You get the idea!

One day the children and I celebrated a new turtle puppet I had received as a gift. We improvised a version of the fable "Tortoise and the Hare." We all danced the slow, determined, disciplined Tortoise and the fast, jumpy, hoppy, smug Hare.

When we danced the Hare, we were so far ahead in the race that we stretched, looked for delicious carrots, and took a break.

As we sat down, munching our invisible carrots, I kiddingly said, "The carrots sat under a tree eating their rabbits." The children rolled over laughing. That line became part of the story, repeated over and over with accompanying giggles each and every time.

When the Tortoise won the race, I offered a play on words: "And the turtle wins by a hair!" One of the children mischievously added, "The hairy turtle wins by a hair!"

And we ended with, "The Hare lost!"

When we give ourselves permission to enjoy the playfulness of the creative process, mixing and matching and mismatching, arranging and rearranging material, we model healthy delight in ideas and relationships. When humor is shared, people feel close to each other. Cohesiveness is strengthened. And emergency shots of humor can relieve tense situations; laughter can minimize anxiety.

With yet another group, I celebrated a variation of the story of the animals receiving gifts from the Creator. We danced all the animals as they rejoiced in the gifts they received. The horses galloped. The birds flew. The kangaroos jumped.

With each new gift we chorused, "The horses got gallops. The birds got wings to fly with. Kangaroos got jumping feet." As the story continued, we added to the chant.

In the middle of the drama, I accidentally bumped Avi on the head with my tambourine. His face changed from smiles to whimpers. Tears in his eyes, lips trembly, he stopped the action. Realizing that he wasn't physically hurt, I patted him and said, "And Avi got a tambourine on his head." Avi fell to the floor laughing. The other children joined him in gales of laughter.

Thus the story developed: "The horses got gallops. The birds got wings to fly with. Kangaroos got jumping feet. Avi got a tambourine on his head. Fish got fins to swim with. Monkeys got tricks. Turtles got shells."

And which part of the story did the children most enjoy? The part that turned Avi's lips from a pout to a grin: "And Avi got a tambourine on his head!"

It's never too late to begin to appreciate and use this very special gift of ours. Remember, we get better at whatever we practice, so begin now to practice enjoying and encouraging the humor within and around you. Talk with children and listen to them. When your daily plan makes room for laughter, you will find yourself and the children learning successfully together in loving ways. Cherish that gift!

Hangin' Out With the Muffin Man

We will enjoy children more and serve them better, as teachers and friends, when we come to appreciate the joys of just hanging out with them—experiencing life through their eyes and ears.

Our Len has so many friends. Michelle is 3, and she's called "Shellie Bellie" or "Boo." Harry's 2. His parents call him "Baby Mon," "Harry Mon," "H Mon B Mon," and "The Hairmeister." Louis is 1. His grandpa and grandma call him "Babalulu" or "Luigi." Callie Rose is 5 months old. Her daddy calls her "Callie Callie Coo." Len is almost 9 months old. He's called "Yummy," "Bunny," "Diddle," and "Munchkin," but our favorite nickname for him is "The Muffin Man," and our favorite activity is hanging out with the Muffin Man.

There are so many things to see when you hang out with the Muffin Man. Big things like buildings and cars.

Little things like buzzing flies, eyes changing expressions, a leaf swaying in the wind. Faraway things like clouds. Close-up things like noses. Exciting things like a traffic light or baggage riding along the airport conveyor belt. Hangin' out with the Muffin Man is a festival of sounds. He listens to sounds that we hardly notice: breezes just beginning, mobiles swinging, faucets dripping.

Life is at our fingertips when we're with the Muffin Man because he reminds us about the fun of touching. Fingers want to hold other fingers, spoons, or flower petals. If he can reach it, he wants to touch it. He grabs at dust particles shining in the bright noon, light in the window, and the flickering of passing shadows.

The Muffin Man thinks that the world is a big red ball waiting for him to grab and bounce, to taste and touch. Everything is on the Muffin Man's menu: dirt, sandpaper, crayons—even food.

Strollering along with the Muffin Man, we talk about so many things. We don't want to miss a second of seeing and being on a walk with, on a talk with, the Muffin Man. It's singing and seeing and saying as we walk with the Muffin Man, chanting names of animals and objects, turning dogs and cats into songs and rhymes and games.

Oh, the patience, persistence, and courage of the Muffin Man! Sitting, crawling, standing, walking. Trying and failing. Pushing and failing. Up, then down, then up again and up, up, up and down and up. Pouts and smiles. Whimpers and laughs. Now, we clap hands. "Peek-a-boo, Muffin Man!"

We lull the Muffin man to sleep after a splashy giggle bath, after hugs in fluffy towels and kisses to shiny clean toes and dimpled fingers, after snuggles and whispers of love, after lullabies and stories and pats on the tush to send him off to sleep with the touch of reassurance. While the Muffin Man sleeps his deep, dreamy sleep in his crib of rainbow colors; in his room of stars, moons, and animals; near his open box of books and toys; we rock in the rocking chair and think about the future.

In a few months Harry starts a new preschool. Michelle will go to pre-K three days a week. Louis will try a play group. Len and Callie may be in a child care program. Some of these children's new friends will also have funny, affectionate nicknames given to them by doting families. Some will be given funny, loving names by the new family of friends they share in their various programs.

But all of our children are coming to you, to school. They will zigzag up a ladder on different rungs—child care, preschool, Head Start. They will hopscotch around from a family child care home to pre-K to play group. Then on to kindergarten, then first grade, and on and on along their journeys from our arms to your arms.

One day you may look up to see a group of children standing before you. Check their names on your roster. Check their knapsacks of unique experiences, talents, and gifts. In the sweet circle of your warmth, they're sure to fall in love with you. Lucky you to be spending time with The Hairmeister, Boo, Luigi, Callie Callie Coo, and their friends. Lucky you to be hanging out with the Muffin Man.

We Drew a Circle That Took Him In

Every teacher has had a child who remains outside the group, giving little sign of interest or involvement in what's going on. To bring that child into the group—not by force, but by patience, caring, and ingenuity—is the challenge.

Randy is in your class. Do you see him, with the half-closed eyes and slumpy back, leaning against the wall when everyone's jumping with the excitement of an idea? Why is his head on the table while other eyes are beaming their brights on you? Randy doesn't respond when you ask a question or seem to be listening when you read a story. What to do about Randy?

Through all my years of working with children, through all the Randys, I have agonized over these questions: Where did we go wrong? How can these children be reached? What can we do to connect with them? The Randys who, in addition to appearing tuned out or turned off, needed more help than their teachers could give were referred to trained psychologists or counselors. But the majority of Randys weren't seen as needing professional treatment. Their teachers viewed them as "indifferent" or "nonparticipating."

Through all these long years, through all the Randys, I have threatened, pleaded, bribed, nudged, cajoled, whimpered, and begged. None of my approaches succeeded in changing silent, nonparticipating Randys into healthy, involved, active children. But as many of us do, I adhered to that age-old practice: If it doesn't work, keep doing it! For years I kept doing it and it hadn't worked, so finally I decided to look at the Randys from a different perspective. I changed my head! I turned on my windshield wipers. I had clearer vision.

The experience of my friend Candace Mazur, who works with Artists-in-the-Schools, reminded me of something I already knew but had forgotten. She saw a nonparticipating Randy standing apart, semi-watching her imaginative troll celebrations with a large group of children. She glanced at that Randy but had no time to do anything special to catch him in her web of enchantment. *Can't win them all,* she thought to herself, and turned her attention back to the group.

That night at the school open house, a couple came toward her gushing with enthusiasm. "Whatever you did today, Candace, you really turned our son on! Why, that boy came home from school, ran to his room, and changed it into a troll's den!" You guessed it. The couple were Randy's parents!

Over the years, I had forgotten that most of our Randys who are half-listening, their flags at half-mast, are really with us. They go home and report on "what we did today." In many cases, parents never know that their children have not demonstrated one gesture of interest.

From my newly discovered insight came a bold new approach. It's based on the following beliefs, and it works!

There is no way any child can be left out of anything we do.

There is no way any child can leave himself out of anything we do.

Even if our Randys are as stiff as lava-covered Pompeii figures or as turned off as electricity in a power failure, in my mind these children are with us. Our circle takes them in. Here's some vocabulary that reflects this way of teaching, used to entice Randys to participate in our movement sessions:

"We need someone to watch the parade. Thanks, Randy . . ."

"Oh, who will be the audience for our circus? Randy, thanks for volunteering!"

"We need someone waiting for the group to come home from the zoo. Randy, will you be the person waiting? Thanks a lot!"

"Randy, will you be the person standing at the corner to let us know when the traffic has passed? Thanks!"

After a while, Randy is bombarded with participation suggestions. Mind you, he hasn't moved one muscle. He hasn't even agreed to the offers. But, because my blood type is B-positive, I believe that he is always participating, appreciated, and needed.

Let me tell you about one particular Randy. It is spring, and this Randy has not budged in my movement sessions with his kindergarten class since September. But, he's never left out. I must confess, however, that over these months I have lost it and resorted sometimes to kidding: "Randy, don't overdo it! Don't strain yourself!" Once in a while, I've tricked him into a trace of a smile.

This has gone on for three seasons. Today, Randy's teacher wants us to enrich our study of nutrition. I am ready with a curriculum.

The kindergartners bounce in. My eyes blink. Am I seeing things? Is Randy bouncing in with the others? I am in shock. Randy is dancing over to me. Randy is excited. Randy bursts with the news!

"Mimi! I can snap!"

Randy's hand is in the air. Randy's fingers snap, crackle, pop. Castanet fingers. Randy is proud. He can't stop snapping.

This calls for an immediate response. A super-structured teacher might say, "That's nice, Randy. But we're not scheduled for snapping until the third week in May. Can you hold your snap?" Or "Randy, this isn't sharing time. Why not wait until next Tuesday's sharing time to show us your snap?" or "Snapping is interesting, Randy, but today we are studying nutrition, so snap out of it!"

But, as you know, creative teachers improvise and invent a lot. I say, "Randy! That is amazing! Are you a mind reader? How did you know that we're doing a story today that desperately needs snapping?"

Randy is hopping with excitement.

I instantly make up a story. We use movement, drama, and music and follow with the children representing the experience in pictures and words.

"Those of you who can snap, get ready. Those who can't, fake it."

We snap our fingers.

"Once upon a time it was raining *(we snap)*. Thundering *(we boom)!* Lightning *(we jab)!* Far from their homes, rabbits were playing. Oh, no! Rain! The rabbits hopped quickly back to their rabbit hutches."

I turn on bouncy music. We all hop back to our shelter.

Randy, the hopping rabbit, moves with his rabbit friends as if he has been moving with them since birth. (Naturally, we always move in the same direction around the room. Safety first!)

"The rabbits reached their shelter. They shook off the rain. They talked in rabbit language translated into English. What do you think they said?"

"I got rain in my ears." (Gretchen)

"My tail is all wet." (Jeremy)

"I hopped in a puddle." (Melissa)

Well, you get the idea. Oops! The teacher is glaring at me. *What happened to nutrition?* she is wondering. Not to worry!

"Well, now the rabbits are ready to sleep. What nutritious snack can they have before bedtime?"

"Carrots!" (Jordan)

"Lettuce!" (Mitchell)

And so the story continues. The rain keeps falling in finger snaps. The thunder and lightning keep thundering and lightning, booming and jabbing. Far from their homes, horses, birds, deer, and children have to gallop, fly, leap, and jog. Of course, when these animals and humans reach their homes and dry off, they all have nutritious snacks. What nutritious snacks can you think of? Well, you get the idea!

The whole session takes 15 minutes—from the class bouncing in, to Randy's snappy announcement, to the story with at least five separate chapters, to the summary of nutritious snacks.

As miraculously as a snake sheds its skin, as Leo the Late Bloomer blooms, Randy the Snapper charged into life. Because Randy had always "participated" in our time together, we couldn't express our monumental astonishment and joy. Because we never let his circles leave us out and always drew circles that took him in, when he actually did jump in, it was just a lovely, everyday event—no big thing.

In my notebook, I scribbled, "From Catatonic to Hyperactive: Randy Snapped Today." No big thing? Then why, after school that day, did the kindergarten teachers and I laugh and cry together?

On Wednesdays
I Can't

All of us—children and adults alike—are still learning. And that means sometimes we're "on," and sometimes we're not. And . . . you can't always predict which we'll be.

It was Wednesday, my day with kindergartners at a nearby school. Oh, what fun to play around with nursery rhymes, Shel Silverstein poems, Winnie-the-Pooh characters, and baby animals in the oldest and most joyful ways—through song, dance, story, laughter, and improvisation! After our bouncy, active session, the children in the last group were getting ready to return to their classroom and continue exploring their ideas in words and pictures. Jimmy walked over to me and asked, "Mimi, could you help me tie my shoes?"

"Sure."

As I bent down to accommodate the request, I heard his voice from above, explaining matter-of-factly, "Some days I can. Some days I can't."

That seemed like a very clear message. I responded, "Me too. Some days I can and some days I can't."

His shoes tied, I stood up. Jimmy looked at me with calm, confident eyes and, before he turned to go, announced, "On Wednesdays I can't."

As the children waved and hugged good-bye, I slapped Jimmy an extra high five. Thank you, I thought, for reminding me of what I sometimes remember and sometimes forget: I am still learning.

Sometimes we can, and sometimes we can't. My neighbor walked three miles on Monday. Today, he admitted, he walked only two. Maybe he didn't sleep well. Maybe it was the humidity.

Howard usually swims his laps in half an hour. Sometimes it takes him longer. On super days, he slashes through the water in 25 minutes.

Cara's handwriting is beautiful—like calligraphy. Once in a while, she scribble-scrabbles a note. "Just lazy," she explains.

Len the Muffin Man is toilet trained. Mostly.

His baby brother, Dylan, sits up by himself. Usually.

Almost always, Callie Callie Coo pronounces her new words clearly. Sometimes she needs an interpreter.

But I think Jimmy has an additional message: *I resist narrow, limited definitions.* Don't stuff me neatly into learning-style systems. Don't think I'm totally predictable.

Don't file us humans away in computer disks—we're full of surprises!

Catch us on a good day and one, two, three, we're awake! Alert! Everything comes together. We're a symphony of synthesis. Test us then. We'll score!

But don't test us on Wednesdays. On Wednesdays we can't.

As We Believe, So We Teach

Does a program, a school, a district determine the curriculum for our classrooms? Maybe. But ultimately, the curriculum we teach depends on what we believe.

I am spending time with two kindergarten classes. The theme in both classes is the circus, and both are using the theme to learn many skills and facts.

Let's visit room A, a very neat and orderly place. On the bulletin board, a large, colorful poster from a resource center features a shiny, smiling circus clown. On the shelves are books about the circus. The children are working quietly at their tables, filling out worksheets about the circus. Those who have finished their seatwork are waiting patiently to begin a clown project. When everyone is ready, the teacher will instruct them in making their clowns. After the worksheets are checked and marked, they'll go into their circus folders, which are already thick with worksheets and papers.

Moving on to room B, we open the door to parade music. On the shelves are books about the circus. Colorful circus mobiles made by the children swing from a rainbow-colored clothesline. An assortment of child-made circus posters decorates the walls. The children's tables have been moved about. Some of the children are cutting and coloring on their own. A few children are in the midst of joint projects—making clay animals and acrobats. The room is abuzz with activity. What's all the excitement? Only two more days 'til the big top! The children are making some of their props and costumes and using others that come already made: Hula-Hoops, balloons, clown masks, wigs, tightropes. It takes a few minutes to find the teacher, who is sitting with her head bent, intent on assisting a group of children as they clarify their third variation for the feature act (it has something to do with monkeys!).

On the nearby wall is a collection of circus words illustrated by cutouts and original drawings. Every day, the children add more words as they think of them.

Both classes share the same curriculum. The same letter went home to all the kindergarten families announcing the theme. But what a difference!

What is the difference?

The difference is the teachers. Room A's teacher has a different belief system than does her colleague in room

B. She believes that learning occurs in a highly structured, teacher-directed, tightly controlled program. Children need to follow directions closely. She doesn't believe in the value of individual decision making, the importance of music, the delight of movement, the challenge of group planning. She isn't comfortable with scribbly pictures and unwieldy walls of words. There's no reason for adding to her vocabulary list. She's happiest when her students are sitting quietly doing seatwork. When they get too wiggly, she'll often say, "If there's any more wiggling, no recess!" She is under pressure from families, the school system, and the state to ensure that her kindergartners are competently prepared for the life of tests and measurements in store for them, and this convinces her that she hasn't the time for all the "monkey business" going on next door. Once you let children move about freely, you lose control. She's sure her class will go wild if she gives them permission to "be" a circus character.

For her class's culmination of the theme, the students will perform a little play about the circus that she found in a children's magazine. As soon as the children finish their clown pictures for the hall bulletin board, they'll rehearse the play. Those who don't have parts will be the audience. They'll wait while the others practice. Her students are used to waiting.

Both rooms have a circus theme. Will *circus* be the same for the children in room A as for those in room B?

We—the teachers—are the curriculum. Not our letters home, not the sayings and slogans we hang on our walls, not the titles and labels carved above our portals or the headlines pinned on our bulletin boards. The curriculum is what's inside. As we believe, so we teach!

And the children know. They can sniff out the truth more sensitively than dogs sniff out a suspicious stranger.

Some of my beliefs:

- I believe in music, one of our first languages and the language of the human spirit. Many babies sing before they speak.

- I believe in movement, our first sign of life. We worry when something stops moving for a long time. It's unhealthy to ask children to sit still for long periods of time.

- I believe in helping children make connections and see relationships.

- I believe in encouraging children to actively participate in their own learning process. Education is a journey with its own timeline, its own unfolding that is unique to each learner.

- I believe that the children who come to our sacred spaces must find challenges, successes, friendships, strengthening, and skills that are fun and taught with creativity, in holistic ways. This begins the love of learning that will last throughout their lives.

- I believe that I need to hurry to the kindergartners in room B. I promised the circus paraders that I would help them with their banner-waving, circus-dancing march.

No Rx for Reading

Children all learn to read a little bit differently . . . yet we still search for that One Way that will work for them all.

O Reading! What is the best way (note the singular *way* instead of plural *ways*) to teach reading to our children? We in education are so frustrated, so polarized. Remember, we live in a fast-food, instant-gratification, high-speed, high-demand inputs-and-outcomes culture. We want more bang for our buck! One size fits all! A newspaper headline reads, "Rx for Better Readers." *Rx* means prescription. Prescription means written order, rule, official law or direction. Prescription means recipe, cure-all, heal-all, command, formula, ordinance.

But there is no single Rx for better readers. Let me tell you about some friends of mine.

Rose

After 30 years of teaching the early grades in public schools, Rose plunged into a daring new adventure—learning Korean. Why? Her network of new, caring Korean friends encouraged her to learn their language so she'd be able to communicate more easily with them and so she'd be prepared when she visited South Korea. Bravely, Rose enrolled in Korean 101 at her university.

Her first lesson was that she was not an auditory learner! Her Korean instructor was used to having 40 to 50 students in his classes back home, and he taught in traditional ways—lecturing, assigning readings in the text, and having students memorize. Some of Rose's classmates (especially those with some prior knowledge of the language) had few problems following along. Others had difficulties. Rose had great difficulties. She was ready to throw in the towel. Urged to keep a journal of this new, challenging experience (Rose had other descriptive words for this immense undertaking), she jotted notes throughout this unprecedented, traumatic quarter.

"I think in different ways. The text is no help at all! I'm walking in like a young child who doesn't yet know the symbols for the different sounds. I feel so stupid! Like quitting. The instructor has no idea of how some of us are struggling. I'm reading letter by letter—the way a lot of kids do. When he tells us a word, I have no carryover that those letters make up that word."

Coming to her rescue, Rose's friends dedicated their time and creativity to help her make sense out of the unfamiliar symbols and sounds. Rushing out for fast-food suppers, Rose's best friend, Sung-Lyul, shaped Korean letters out of French fries. Throughout those first weeks, her friends made letters out of their fingers, drew story maps to clarify meanings, used dramatically exaggerated gestures and voices to help her comprehension, and improvised songs that helped her vocabulary.

"I definitely would have dropped the class if not for Sung-Lyul and my friends coming to the rescue," she wrote. "Just like Home Support! Now I understand why so many children give up when they're having difficulties and no one at home is there for them. But kids can't drop the course. They drop their spirit and just sit there, not learning."

As the quarter went on, Rose learned a lot, but she also helped her instructor learn. He slowed down, made more time for questions, encouraged more, loosened up.

"When I read the new word today, my instructor said, 'Good!' It meant so much to me and I remember my years of teaching children and thought how important it is to keep in mind those little (immense?) accomplishments and take time to celebrate them. Those moments motivate the learner to continue with the struggle."

It took over a month for Rose to crack the code of the three basic vowel symbols.

"I cried. I felt frustrated. Here I am, a teacher, trying to find techniques to help myself. I'm as frustrated as that little first grader, and I'm armed with ways of learning!"

Thanks to french fries, fingers, drama, improvised songs, and a more flexible teacher, Rose is now reading simple Korean stories and menus. She can have brief conversations with Korean friends (if they speak slowly), can recognize more words than she can say, and feels very proud of herself but also deeply humbled:

"I wish I'd had this experience before I taught children for 30 years. I would have been much more empathetic—more aware of the different ways children learn, the different ways we all learn. This experience gave me deeper insight into that complicated process called learning."

Umberto and Domenico

Vesna explains her family this way: "We are parents from two different cultures living in a third culture with children getting educated in a fourth culture!" Her children, Umberto (3½) and Domenico (2-ish), wave a cheery goodbye to Vesna as they run to their teachers at the Jewish Center's early childhood program. The two brothers speak and understand Macedonian, which they learned from their mother and her family. With their dad, Giuseppe, they speak Italian. English is the language they speak with their friends and their mom. In school, they are learning Hebrew songs and words. At very young ages, Umberto and Domenico are trilingual with a touch of a fourth language!

They love books. Story time is a special time. Most of the books Vesna reads to them are in English. The boys know how books work—left to right, print and pictures moving the stories along. Almost always, because they love their story time, they beg Vesna, "Read it again, Mama" (and again, and again).

When their Uncle Kris returned home from a trip to Macedonia, bringing children's books to his nephews, the children's grandparents read them the new gifts. Sitting on their grandparents' laps, the boys followed along in Macedonian, looking at the Macedonian text. When the stories were over, the boys would beg in Macedonian, "Read it again, Dedo [Grandpa]. Read it again, Baba [Grandma]!"

Whenever Vesna works at her desk at home, the boys set up their desks and busily write their reports and letters. They have a box filled with the hieroglyphics of toddlers. When their Uncle Kris was in Macedonia, Umberto concentrated on a very special letter. He read the letter (written in scribble-scrabble) to his mom:

"Dear Uncle Kris. I miss you very much."

Soon the boys' noodly letter shapes will transform into recognizable letters. The Roman alphabet used by English and Italian will probably emerge first, followed by the Cyrillic alphabet that Macedonians use. Most certainly, the children will recognize the designs of Hebrew letters from posters and pictures in school. When mail arrives from their Italian grandparents across the ocean, Umberto and Domenico will have no trouble remembering to deliver those letters to their father, Guiseppe.

This is a hang-loose time in their lives and they are living it up! No one is pushing them, drilling them to learn the letters in any of their three languages. Their teachers, parents, and friends know that any minute Umberto will write a few words in English, Macedonian, or Italian when he writes another letter to his Uncle Kris.

Ben

Please don't disturb Ben. He's finishing *The Phantom Toll Booth*. Ben is 5 years old.

Excuse me—5 years old and reading *The Phantom Toll Booth?* How did this happen?

All we know is that Ben's family and caregivers have been reading to Ben since he was an infant. But haven't many of our children been read to since birth?

Ben was an early talker. At 20 months, he loved pointing to letters and words and delighted in naming the letters. His favorite words at 1½ were names of cars, which he identified by colors, styles, and even their owners: "That's a Mommy car—Volvo!"

When his mom bought a set of magnetic letters, he not only knew the names of all of them but played jokes to trick people, like taking out the *M* and replacing it with a *W*.

At 2, he pointed out syllables and words on the pages of books that were read to him. He even read contractions correctly, saying "do not" instead of "don't." Riding in the car, he asked his mom, "What's 'one way'?" as they passed the road sign.

When he was 2½, he was reading. If you handed him a Dr. Seuss book that he had never seen, he could read it.

At the zoo with his Aunt Marlene, Ben read the signs giving information about the animals. He was just 3 years old.

How Ben learned to read is still a mystery.

Scientists don't know exactly how children like Ben make sense out of the symbols that form words and make meanings. Meanwhile, millions of parents and teachers are reading books trying to figure out how to help their children learn to read.

O Reading! There is no Rx for teaching you. We don't even have to teach children like Ben. These mystery children sit in their toddler seats in the back of your car and ask you, "What does 'one way' mean?" As you almost steer off the road, you realize that your 2-year-old has learned to decode the language all by himself, without any conscious help from you!

Children who learn like Rose need fingers, songs and games, maps and pictures, clay, sand, and blocks to help them get along on this incredible adventure.

Umberto and Domenico are good listeners. They learn easily, quickly, from tuning in to the sounds and music and rhythms of words and language. Gestures, facial expressions, and movement patterns help them on this wondrous journey.

Children reflect and celebrate the multiple intelligences of the human family. They learn to read by a combination of many print-surrounded, print-immersed experiences: from puppets to posters, from creative movement to field trips, from storytellers to storytelling to story writing to story reading. We learn in so many different ways, on so many different levels. Learning is a multidimensional, continuous, ever-evolving experience. No single Rx (no matter what its value) succeeds with all children.

We do know a few things. Children need to be welcomed into the world of language at birth. They need to be talked to, sung to, read to, included in the richness of language from infancy on. Children who grow up in lonely environments, with minimum interaction and communication, who rarely see examples of print, who don't get lulled to sleep with lullabies and dazzled by stories, who have no one to walk along or talk along with them, will have problems learning how to read. They, as do all children, desperately need exciting, joyful, fun-filled early childhood programs rich in loving, dynamic learning moments and methods.

Get out the french fries and spell No Rx for Better Readers.

Get the Elephant Out of the Room
We're Finished With the Es!

Despite all their textbooks and notebooks packed with information, despite the research and scholarship available to them, teachers and education students are always astonished at the daily situations that their courses of study didn't cover—situations that demand a combination of spontaneity, imagination, boldness, instinct, faith, and playfulness to guarantee intelligent and loving responses.

Shiggy started it all when he wore his new firefighter's hat to his class's first movement session in September. He and his toddler colleagues came zooming into the dance room all fired up about fires. It was such a hot subject! How could I fight such enthusiasm?

Scrapping my plan to celebrate the folk tune "Old Mac-Donald Had a Farm" with music, dance, improvisation, animal dialogue, humor, and drama, I switched to the teacher version of automatic pilot (in other words, winging it) and created a story about firefighters: "Once upon a time the firefighters were sleeping in the firehouse." (The children dropped to the floor, closed their eyes, and snored. Debbie, their good-sport teacher, tiptoed to the corner of the room. At my signal, she burst into arm-waving, finger-vibrating, torso-swaying flames. I sounded the alarm.)

"The firefighters jumped up, dressed quickly, slid down the pole, and hurried to their fire trucks!" I continued. (The children accompanied the narrative with rapidly changing movement patterns, demonstrating dressing, sliding, rushing.)

"Sirens blaring, the fire trucks raced round the city to the fire." (We always practice moving around the room in the same direction. This safety habit is deeply instilled in all the children I work with. On this day, the fire trucks raced around the city to the bouncy beats of exciting Israeli/Arab music. Because we always have the music of the world at our fingertips, we play the music of the world with all new ideas.)

"The firefighters arrived at the fire. They *uncurled* their hoses, *stretched* their ladders, *climbed up,* and *balanced* themselves as they aimed their heavy power hoses toward the flames. Finally, the fire was out!" (The fiery Debbie slowly drooped to the floor. The firefighters and I hoorayed. To the percussive rhythms of African drums and bells, the fire engines raced back to the firehouse.)

Before I could steer us on to Old MacDonald's farm, as I had planned, the children sang out, "Can we do that again? Can we have another fire?" (Confession: I am a person who lets children boss her around—especially when they are enthralled with an idea. I call the ideas children are madly in love with *magic vocabulary*. Obviously, *fire* was at the top of Shiggy and his classmates' magic vocabulary list.)

That day we extinguished three major fires. One of them happened on Old MacDonald's farm. Debbie got triple aerobics points as she flared and flamed in different locations around the room.

"Is this in my job description?" she joked. "I'm almost burnt out!"

From that day on, Shiggy and his classmates continued rushing to every single movement session with their zealous chant, "Can we do the fire story?"

I never brought up the word *fire* to these children, yet they always requested the firefighters' story. Whoever believes that young children have short attention spans needs to spend time with a group of young children when they're immersed in a fascinating subject.

Confronted with this weekly challenge, I realized that my choices were limited to three:

1. Burn all my plans and curriculum guides.
2. Sweetly say, "Enough is enough already with the fires! We need to get on with our other very important work!"
3. Be creative, imaginative, flexible, open-minded, playful, holistic, courageous, tuned in to the children, and brilliant, and figure out ways to link fire to every other subject or topic. In other words, make connections.

Naturally I chose number three, over and over again. Shiggy's class did not miss a chance to work with a fire story; we integrated fires and firefighters in every session. We put out fires in all kinds of places:

- On Old MacDonald's farm
- On the Yellow Brick Road (didn't poor Scarecrow almost catch fire?)
- At the circus (all those torches and fireworks)
- On the property of the Three Pigs (remember when the wolf slid down the chimney into a pot of boiling water and burned his tush?)
- In the rain forest (forest fires are very dangerous)
- On the road with Jack Be Nimble (better jump very high over that candlestick, Jack!)

Have I made the point, or are more examples necessary?

Education is a dynamic, exciting, elusive, and mysterious process. You're either open or closed. You're either flexible or uptight. You're either integrated or compartmentalized. Which side are you on?

Over the decades, I have experienced hundreds of incidents in which very structured, inflexible teachers slammed shut doors that would have led to opportunities for joyful learning. They have said:

"It's not in my lesson plan."

"I didn't have enough advance notice."

"It doesn't fit into our schedule."

"It's not included in our curriculum."

"We've already finished studying that."

But aren't the moments we remember most clearly the ones that simply *happened*, like Shiggy's firefighter story?

Fire hats off to those creative teachers who put a marker in their daily plan books and embark with their children on adventures into uncharted territories! They improvise new combinations, discover amazing connections. The powerful elements of surprise, delight, appreciation, and comprehension dazzle the participants.

To such experiences, we bring everything that is in us as teachers—and even more. (Do we really know *all* of our gifts and resources?) The children contribute their best energy and ideas. Language flows and grows in these shared times when we are learning together on the journey.

One particular February was a weird month for weather. The temperature rose into the 40s and 50s, ruining a kindergarten teacher's plan (marked "snow and snowpeople" in bold print in her planner book). She always saves *snow* for what is usually the coldest month. She bases her activities and projects on bundling up and playing out in the snow. She could have been the kind of teacher who is rigid even when the month of February is not frigid! But she isn't. She could have said, "These are my well-prepared, carefully thought out plans. Even though the air is warm and there is no snow on the ground, we are going to follow these activities to the letter. They were good enough for the last 10 Februaries and they will be good enough for now. Business as usual!"

But she didn't. Instead, with a twinkle in her eye and a hang-loose sense of humor, she shared an idea for a new twist on the snow activities with her kindergartners. "How about if we put swimsuits on our snowpeople?"

Giggling, the children celebrated snow figures and snow games, but the context and content were original. They listened to their teacher explain, "Boys and girls, if this was a regular, old-fashioned February, we would be surrounded by snow. Let's talk about snow!" And they did. They talked about statistics and weather records and average temperatures. They discussed comparisons, expectations, and patterns. They learned about graphs and weather reports and predictions.

And the children enjoyed the planned activities and the fun-filled changes that enriched their awareness of how unusual the weather patterns of this particular month were. Their playful pictures expressed the new combinations.

Serendipity plays a large part in the creative process. How do we seize the unexpected opportunities presented to us? Teachers who do not teach in the key of life have told me:

"We don't need to look for comets because we're not up to our space unit yet."

"When Sean brought in the small totem his grandmother carried for him from Alaska, I told him he had to wait his turn for show-and-tell. And he wasn't scheduled for another week. Besides, we don't really study Alaska this year."

At an inservice workshop I presented, "Teaching in the Key of Life," many beginning and experienced teachers expressed concern about handling spontaneous, serendipitous challenges. (It's easier to simply dismiss the opportunities presented!)

I made up a story about a circus animal handler walking an elephant into a nearby elementary school. The two stood in the doorway of a classroom, waiting for the teacher to invite them in.

"Pardon me," the teacher told the animal handler politely. "Could you please take the elephant out of the room? We're finished with the letter *E!*"

At our workshop, from *A* to *Z,* we brainstormed ways to welcome the elephant!

Uh-oh, here comes Shiggy's class! Today's plan is to have a big Presidents' Day celebration. No doubt the fire department will lend us a few fire engines and firefighters to lead the festivities. What's a parade without a fleet of fire trucks?

We never know when that fire alarm will go off, do we?

My Puppet Needs Ritalin

Puppets can help us see things—and children—just a little bit differently.

Snowball, my "main squeeze" brown-and-white puppy puppet, has accumulated thousands of frequent flier miles in our travels around the country to hang out with teachers and children of all ages. Wherever we go, he's a hit!

In our movement, music, and story times at a community center in Columbus, Ohio, Snowball sometimes makes an appearance and tells me (only I can hear him!) his favorite part of the story or idea we just celebrated. I tell the children what he says. For example, if we create a story and dance for *Goldilocks and the Three Bears,* Snowball might tell me his favorite part of the story was when the wolf huffed and puffed but couldn't blow the house down.

He *always* goofs it up! He is courteous, sweet-tempered, and interested, but he doesn't pay attention. He's easily distracted. Even blanket-clutching, homesick toddlers burst into peals of laughter at some of Snowball's off-the-wall responses. They love him and enjoy correcting him.

"Snowball," they cheerily scold, "pay attention!"

On other occasions in his role as member of the Medical Emergency Squad, Snowball rushes to aid a fallen child.

"Where does it hurt?" I ask for Snowball.

The usually *not* hurt but startled child will point to an arm or a leg.

"Snowball will kiss Tyler's boo-boo," I prescribe. And he plants mushy kisses on Tyler's nose or the top of his head, while tears dry and are replaced by giggles.

Tyler corrects the medic: "No, Snowball! Not my head—my leg! Pay attention!"

One treatment from Snowball and most injuries are immediately healed.

When a more reluctant class comes into our space (children get into moods, too, right?), I call on Snowball to help motivate the group into action.

Snowball whispers into my ear. I convey the message.

"Hey, friends, Snowball doesn't think you guys are in great shape today. I told him you were high jumpers and fast runners, but he doesn't believe me. Shall we show him?"

"Okay!" More than okay! Our droopy-eyed slouchers straighten up and take off around the room in the same direction. I put the music on. Any rhythmic music from anywhere in the world will do. Round and round the room they run.

"Put the music in your feet," I call. We run, run, run, then we jump, jump, jump. Run-run-run-jump-jump-jump until we fall down!

While the children lie on the floor catching their breath, I ask Snowball, "What do you think of our super-fit-as-a-fiddle children now?"

Snowball flops his ears and claps his paws in glee, full of excitement. Then he whispers in my ear. I tell the children, "Snowball says that was cool. Can you do it again?"

The exhausted children, still catching their breath, shout, "No way!"

"We're tired and ready for a story," Jake explains.

I lower my voice in confidence to the group. "You know how eager and excited, how hyper, Snowball is. Should we do our whole running and jumping exercise for him again?"

"Snowball, I think you should be on Ritalin!" Evan advises. As his classmates agree, Snowball bounces, wiggles, and flops his ears.

"I think he's so excited and happy to be with you today," I say.

The children chime in to tell about their friends and family members who take medication.

We dance and sing our story, and when we say good-bye, Snowball reappears and gives good-bye kisses. Now, these are 4- and 4½-year-olds, many of whom have known Snowball from their early childhood education programs in infant and toddler groups. This day, Audrey runs back to share a momentous discovery she just made.

"Mimi, I think Snowball is a puppet!"

Between waves of laughter I reassure her, "He *is* a puppet, honey!"

Looking at him meaningfully for a second, she hugs him, gives him a sweet good-bye kiss, and runs to catch up with her class.

Snowball and I have an appointment at the doctor's, and Snowball will probably have to be tested. Unfocused, silly random responses; overly enthusiastic behavior; not recognizing limits; and confusing comprehension can mean only one course—medication!

We might have to go for a second opinion!

Education Is a Moving Experience

Children are eager to be invited to experience learning that is joyful, meaningful, relevant, and multilayered. Connecting movement to all the areas of the curriculum, to all skills, is natural, for the arts are the connective tissue that holds our spirits intact.

Rain falls. Sun shines. Planets revolve. Earth turns. Fire burns. Volcanoes erupt. Gingerbread men run. Flowers grow. Clowns juggle. Frogs jump. Monkeys swing. Conestoga wagons roll. Flags unfurl. Ships sail. Archaeologists dig. Winds blow. Continents shift. Peacocks strut. Tornadoes spin.

Thank you, Howard Gardner, for legitimizing movement, music, dance, drama, and play as basic ways of learning in your wonderful multiple intelligences theory.

We who work and play with children day by day and year by year have always known that for so many people, the most effective ways to learn, comprehend, absorb, and know is through movement, music, and kinesthetic experiences. And research supports the value of diverse learning methods.

It's all about making connections—about helping children (and ourselves) see relationships. Learning isolated skills and facts in static settings just doesn't cut it. Every idea, lesson, and concept can be enriched by movement, by dance. Without the arts as part of our lives, we would be truly handicapped.

The arts help us make the world whole. The arts are our oldest way of learning, expressing ourselves, and communicating. Our ancestors painted masterful pictures on cave walls—some preserved in ancient caves—and crafted amulets, tools, and musical instruments. Their paintings tell their stories. Animals were prominent subjects, but look carefully and you will see dancers and ceremonies and people caught in action. In many tribal cultures, there is no word for art. The arts are part of everything! Seasons, events, places, life passages, community traditions—the arts are the core way people honor important ideas and happenings. Children learn their culture through the arts.

No matter what grade, age, or subject you teach, think connections. Draw a circle. In the center of the circle, in the hub, draw the children and the idea you want to convey. Then draw many spokes coming out from the hub. Write *dance, music, story, drama, poetry,* and *visual arts* on the spokes. Don't leave out the standard curriculum areas, such as reading, math, science, and social studies. All will connect to the central idea, to the children learning in their best, most successful combination of ways. And remember, movement, dance, and music are very old ways. If your environment is one of trust and love, the words *show me* will be magical words that inspire children to respond with bodies in shapes and motion.

During the many years I've been bouncing around the education field, we've danced and moved to depict people escaping slavery and finding safety stations on their way to freedom; Apollo's chariot galloping across the sky, carrying the sun; all the king's horses and men racing to help Humpty Dumpty; caterpillars transforming to butterflies, tadpoles transforming to frogs; a cold front moving in, heavy with molecules; seasons performing their dynamic pageant; the wheels of the bus rumbling their way to the zoo; our understanding of number facts and spelling words, the parts of speech, and famous speeches.

As we believe, so we teach. If we believe music, dance, poetry, chant, mime, visual arts, and drama are separate and sometimes unequal human activities having little relationship to anything else, that's the narrow message we'll transmit to children.

If we believe all concepts, topics, and themes have countless built-in dimensions of learning, we will help children make discoveries, delight in surprise, and celebrate comprehension as they grow in awareness, knowledge, and skills.

On the way home from his preschool program, 2½-year-old Micah told his mommy about his morning.

She asked him, "How was movement with Mim?"

He said, "I helped Mim today."

"How?" asked Mom.

"I jumped!"

Remember, education is a moving experience. Get moving!

Uh-Uh! None of This "I'm Not Creative" Stuff

Dedicated to Sylvia Ashton-Warner's wonderful reminder that before we teach others, we must teach ourselves.

You say you're not creative!

You shrink away from that "c" word. Well, I'm here to tell you that you *are* creative. Listen up!

You are a member of a very creative family. You're not a green bean, a lima bean, a baked bean, or a kidney bean. You're a human bean, and you have been given a gift of creativity as part of your heritage, your legacy, your designer genes!

Don't limit your interpretation of that "c" word to the making of a creative product like a poem, dance, or painting. That "c" word encompasses process as well as product. It has to do with a way of thinking, of being, of living.

It's about flexibility, spontaneity, serendipity, openness, playfulness, experimentation, exploration, connections, combinations, changes, rearranging, and arranging.

Whenever you walk up to a salad bar and fill your plate with a selection of the offerings, you participate in a creative act. Think about it. Do all the plates held by all the customers look exactly the same after they are filled with salad items? Of course not. Each plate is an expression of a unique individual.

Visit a high-rise apartment building where each unit has exactly the same layout. Knock on every door. Even though the floor plans are identical, are all the apartments designed and decorated exactly the same? Of course not. Each dwelling space is an expression of a unique individual.

Check out a flower shop or greenhouse. Note the contents of passing shopping carts. Each reflects the individual taste, interests, and decision making of the owner. Wander around looking at people's gardens. Note the variety of designs and layouts. Admire the color explosions of wildflowers and contrast them with the pristine, orderly, monochromatic pattern of just one type of flower.

Every day you make countless decisions that reflect the uniquely human spirit of creativity. Can we become more aware of such a precious gift? You bet we can!

Enjoy these four hints, four little exercises (aerobics for the mind) to strengthen your creative powers, just for plain fun.

The first hint is to train yourself to ask yourself (and the children you work with), "What else?" No matter what you're doing, thinking, or planning, whisper, "What else?" to yourself, and your brain will begin whirling: What else can we add to this idea? What else can we combine? What else will connect? What else can we think of for our party? trip? theme? reunion? poem? story? program? When you ask "What else?," you help dissolve the negative, close-minded, shrinking smugness of "It's finished!" or "We've already done that!" or "I can't think of anything else!" Boo to those enemies of creativity! Train yourself to be open, courageous, willing to be playful, experimental, willing to be surprised. Asking "What else?" kindles the flames of delight and discovery, such important components of the creative process.

The second hint is the question, "What if?" I call these two words the words of wonder. What if you turned your room into a rain forest? an ocean? a time machine? What if you could understand the language of animals? What if you could communicate with your ancestors? What if you could be invisible? The question "What if?" is, as all great questions are, limitless in its possibilities. "What if?" is inspiration for the imagination. "What if?" will take you on marvelous exciting journeys you may need to record, illustrate, map, sketch, paint, dance, sing, describe, dramatize (I could go on . . . and on . . .).

Moving on to our third hint: "Show the idea!" Howard Gardner, in his multiple intelligences theory, helps strengthen our thinking in this most fascinating area. We humans have so many ways to *show* an idea! We aren't limited to instinctual patterns. We have language, visual arts, and kinesthetic awareness. We are poets, builders, dancers, architects, construction workers, philosophers. We can express or communicate an idea in countless ways—why be limited to just one or two? Show your idea using a poster, a chart, a T-shirt, a bumper sticker, a mobile, a book, a construction, a sand sculpture, or a song. Free yourself. Mess around with ideas. Be playful. Be open to the myriad possibilities.

This last hint may seem frivolous, but trust me, it's truly helpful: "If you think you can't do it, pretend you can." Fake it! Try it. Just do it. This is about courage. Don't shrivel your spirit with self-defeating excuses. Risk! Experiment! Be willing to make the effort without fear of criticism or self-doubt or ridicule (enemies of creativity). Surprise yourself. Set a great example for the children you work with. "I'm not Walt Whitman or Langston Hughes or Edna St. Vincent Millay, but I'm going to have a great time trying my hand at writing poetry. Join me! I'm going to pretend I can write a poem! . . . Wow! Did I write that? Not bad!"

Life is short. Fill it with memorable, exciting moments. Encourage children to live their lives to the fullest, to enjoy the ordinary, everyday, miraculous opportunities life offers us to be the most we can. I tell the children (borrowing from the United Negro College Fund's wonderful motto), "Our minds, time, and talents are terrible things to waste!" Expand your thinking about that "c" word. It's an integral part of your identity, your self.

Surprise yourself. And, if you think you can't, fake it!

It's Hard to Smile With a Binky in Your Mouth

Because we work closely with young children, we have the privilege of witnessing everyday miracles . . . like 2-year-olds yielding their most precious treasures to the pull of love!

Decades ago, when I answered a lifelong calling to education, it was unheard of for infants and toddlers to be cared for in structured, formal programs. These days, few blink at 6-week-old newly borns launching their early education journeys in a neighborhood child care home, a classroom in the basement of a church, or a ready-for-action, state-of-the-art, brag-about new child care facility.

True, many of our very youngest children adapt easily to a program when welcomed by loving, warm, joyful, trustworthy teachers. But even with stellar staff members and ideal learning environments—a safe and loving community, delightful developmentally appropriate activities—some very young children take separation from home painfully. They challenge us to constantly reassure them, and nothing seems to diminish their weepy, hesitant, fearful behavior.

For example, meet a few 2s. Binky in her mouth, Shelley will not move without her blankie—worn, torn, and draped or fastened around her body. It is her life jacket. Franklin wears a baseball cap, insists on wearing his backpack at all times, and always clenches his Binky in his teeth. When his class comes into my joyful, musical, bouncy space, he is in his teacher's arms, tears rolling down his cheeks, holding on for dear life. Brianna, with a pink Binky and blankie, makes a fashion statement of color coordination. But even to the casual passerby, these objects of attachment make another clear statement.

In this program I have welcomed seven sessions a week of children, from infants and toddlers to seasoned 4- and 5-year-olds. I am the dancing, moving, musical, playful teacher who has enjoyed seeing almost all of the children eagerly running, skipping, and giggling to my smiley room. (Almost all!) Sometimes my beloved brown-and-white puppy puppet, Snowball, is the welcomer. He sits against the wall and watches the action-filled sessions. At the end of our time together, he distributes kisses to every child. It's always a love fest with teachers, assistant teachers, children, and yours truly enjoying the fun of being together. Every ordinary moment is special!

But let's focus on Shelley, Franklin, and Brianna. Binkies in mouths, backpacks on backs, blankies in hands, these three toddlers have been consistently nonparticipatory for months. They are like small clouds of glumness in a swirl of cheerful, playful, jumping beans.

By May of the school year, the children, teachers, and I have danced, sung, and laughed together through these many weeks. Even the shyest children soon learn that ours is a safe and joyful place to be. And what about our most hesitant holdouts, Shelley, Franklin, and Brianna? Yes, eventually even they feel the love permeating our shared times. Somehow, the relentless warmth has helped melt layers of inhibition and fear. Could it be the continuous bombardment of fun shared through the months? We checked textbooks for answers and found no formula for such situations. The closest wisdom we discovered was words on a poster from an anonymous source: "Whatever the question, the answer is love."

Today is very special. It's that kind of day in the life of those of us who spend time hanging around young children. This crazy field of early childhood education yields many rewards—most not obvious to the general public. Those outside would not recognize the many tiny miracles that happen every day that surprise and astonish us. Miracles like today!

Shelley, Franklin, Brianna, and the other children in their group bounce into my room, ready for dancing, ready for fun. When I see Shelley's worn blankie and Brianna's fashion-pink one, something possesses me to kneel down and ask, "Friends, Snowball is cold today. Do you think you could let him snuggle with your blankies?"

The blankie girls look hard at Snowball, who is wagging his ears merrily, think a minute, and with great courage, nod their heads and hand over their blankies. Just like that! It is hard to hide my astonishment.

We who call ourselves early childhood professionals know these moments. They inspire yelps of release, tears of success, and cheers of undescribed victory that must be stifled. For we must respond in ordinary, undramatic, everyday voices with "Thanks, dear friends. Snowball will be warm now that you have shared your blankies."

On this day, however, such an event calls for a special celebration. "Let's have a parade!" Children love parades, for any or all reasons, or for none.

"We'll need clowns, musicians, and animals in our parade," I suggest. "It's such a beautiful spring day. Let's have a fun parade!" I do not even look at Franklin, Brianna, or Shelley when I say, "Wouldn't it be fun to shout 'Hooray!' And be sure to smile and wave at everyone. Gosh, if you have a Binky in your mouth, it will be hard to smile. Any of you with a Binky in your mouth, can you put it carefully on the blankets with Snowball? He'll watch them for you. We'll wait for you before the parade starts."

Looking intently at one another, our Binky trio of children, one by one, remove the Binkies from their mouths (an almost surgical procedure), walk slowly to the blankie-safe Snowball, and carefully set down their precious possessions.

We teachers begin the parade. This time there are three true reasons to cheer! Every one of those 2-year-olds sings, waves, gallops, and jumps in a parade of delight—with smiles on every face. You would never know that three of the children have not moved this way in all of the past nine months. I suspect that even our veteran puppy, Snowball, is grinning, sensing the immensity of the drama unfolding before him. No passerby could know that one of those many miracles that happen in early childhood teaching is happening right here and now.

Months of constant, consistent, and unswerving fun, love, and reassurance must be part of the answer to whatever the questions. We are still working to understand the underlying reasons for such a moment of change on this wonderful day in May. Guaranteed formulas are not to be found! Perhaps the biggest lesson learned is that *it's hard to smile with a Binky in your mouth.*

Bluegrass and Belly Dance
Dancing With Babies

When very young children see adults filled with free-spirited joy, they begin to connect music, song, and dance to happy times together. What greater life lesson could we help them learn?

Every group of children in the early childhood program I am working in comes to my multipurpose space to dance, laugh, sing, and bounce with me. The 3- and 4-year-olds love to dance to nursery rhymes, nursery stories, parades, holiday songs, and favorite songs that move them, like "Shoo Fly," "Itsy Bitsy Spider," and "Comin' Round the Mountain." They have a plethora of joyful ideas to celebrate, and we *do* each week.

And then there are the infants. I am amazed and amused by our tiniest children, some as young as 6 weeks.

We spread blankets on the floor and set them down, some on their tummies, some on their backs. Some are not yet ready to turn themselves over. A few can sit up by themselves without falling. Some are cuddled on the laps of their wonderful teachers.

During the first weeks of the school year, the babies enter my more unfamiliar, larger space with one of three basic reactions: crying, smiling, or staring at me with unblinking eyes. My first goal: Change the crying to smiling, or at least staring! Usually this can be accomplished with the magic of movement. When the music starts, I dance (improvising, of course), with my limbs, head, legs, and hips—all the moving parts!—in action. The babies are as mesmerized as if they are watching trapeze artists swing from the high wires. I always invite teachers who are not holding an infant to join my dance. The infants are double-mesmerized!

Over those early weeks, I play *everything:* beloved songs like "The More We Get Together" or "Zippity Doo Dah" or "You Are My Sunshine," and rhythmic music from around the world. If the babies do not smile, do not stop crying, or look distracted, I instantly cut off that music, even if it is my very favorite piece (weep), and I try something different.

It's obvious when the babies like the music. You don't need an official evaluation process or an advanced degree in arts education to figure it out. Just *look* and note what you observe. How babies respond to music and rhythm is very unique and diverse. Some babies sway. Some tap. Some kick. Some bounce. Some watch, deciding how or if they want to move. They get good ideas as they see teachers dancing and their friends moving. They catch the joy!

After a while, the babies grow more used to our space, to me, to the idea that we have so much fun together. During these weeks I have introduced the rhythms of the world, from rock and roll to reggae to klezmer to African and Native American drums. Again, if some babies are still frowning or staring, I change the music immediately.

One day we had a major breakthrough—for the first time, *all* of the infants, every single one of them, danced, bounced, tapped, kicked, swayed, smiled, or even laughed! What was the music that caught each child? An old, worn album of bluegrass songs and an old, worn album of belly dance music. I wish we had a video of the three sessions of babies partying like the best festival! Little feet kicking. Tiny hands clapping. Miniature palms tapping. Heads swaying. I will leave it to more scholarly minds to research the exact reason the rhythms of belly dance music and the twanging banjos and guitars of bluegrass so delighted these infants.

Is this a story of what *you* should do with your group of infants and toddlers? No. This is a sharing of a wonderful day with three groups of adorable infants and young toddlers who, for some mysterious reason, felt free, safe, trusting, and open to the rhythms of these cultures. Can we take this for granted? No. Tomorrow I may play this music and the response might be minimal. There are no formulas. The only strategy is to try everything, especially music *you* love, music with rhythms that can be easily accompanied by movement. Turn off what is not stimulating to the children. Consistently provide an atmosphere of joyful welcoming and sharing.

I love to watch the babies as they enjoy our time together. But, it takes time! Be patient and full of faith and courage as you journey these often uncharted paths. We humans are unique beings, with our own particular mix of characteristics and preferences. Even our youngest (not even on earth a year) have their own timetables, their own honest responses and ways of expressing themselves. Patience and hope are important qualities of successful teaching.

I must hurry now. The 3s and 4s are on their way to the multipurpose room. They need no preparation for their sessions of music, dance, and story play—after all, they started falling in love with the joy of music and dance when they were infants. Now they are dancing into the room!

Jamie Burped!

Every day we face situations both BIG—things we need to address—and small—things we can let pass. Let's be wise enough to recognize the difference.

A group of 4-year-olds were hanging out in the informal play area of an early childhood center. When I stopped to greet them with, "What's happening, friends?," I was given some serious information.

"Mimi, Jamie burped!"

I was taken aback by this news and immediately looked at Jamie, whose eyes were downcast, posture crumpled in humiliation.

"Jamie," I asked, "did you burp?"

He nodded guiltily. The others waited for the obviously expected scolding.

"Hey, kids," I smiled, "Guess what? People burp some-times!"

Jamie looked up like a death-sentenced prisoner just pardoned by the governor moments before his execution.

Calling the children around me, I challenged them: "Take a few minutes, please, all of you, and discuss whether you think burping is a BIG THING or a little thing."

They huddled for a while deep in conversation. A few minutes later, they presented their unanimous decision.

"Burping is a little thing."

I congratulated them for having such an important discussion. All smiles, they waved goodbye and returned to their game. Jamie's bright eyes blinked happily as he joined his friends.

Shortly after this incident, I spoke with a group of education majors in the midst of their student teaching assignments. Four of the future teachers were working with mentors in the same building—a large, urban school attended by many Spanish-speaking children from low-income backgrounds. Three of these student teachers raved about their mentor teachers, who were loving, fun, competent, creative, and patient with the children. The fourth hardly spoke. When I asked if she had similar positive experiences, she hesitated and then finally blurted out, "The children are beautiful—fun and funny, smart, so eager to learn. Their teacher is so strict! She's on them for *everything!* 'Pick up that paper . . . Sit up straight . . . Where is your pencil? . . . Don't hold the book *that* way . . .' When I come in," she shyly added, "the kids are so happy to see me. I think it's because someone is smiling at them, greeting them, and not scolding them for everything."

In the conversation that followed, I pointed out that even a negative teaching placement is valuable. It helps confirm your beliefs, values, and commitments. Spending each day with a grim, overly strict teacher brings into focus behavior you want to avoid. Nothing beats firsthand experience and observation.

When I left the meeting with the university students, I thought about my years of required courses, readings, research papers, and lectures in preparation for a career in teaching. Now, after many years in the field, I've concluded that teachers face numerous situations on a daily basis that are not included in that strenuous preparation for this (I call it a sacred calling) profession. So much of what happens demands an instant response, and the way we respond to the myriads of often unexpected concerns is almost instinctive. Our words, actions, body language, and facial expressions reflect our truest state of being.

Many years ago I imagined a little scenario: Each morning we wake to find a voting booth in our beds. Only two parties are running—Life and Death. Almost the second we awake, we vote. If we vote Death, everything is negative, unbearable, frustrating. If we vote Life, we feel lucky to be alive, ready for the new day—open, flexible, welcoming of the day's events. The good news is that we don't just vote once. Every single time we face a decision, we vote. Let me demonstrate this point with three true incidents.

Mark has terrible handwriting. Almost illegible. His teacher could easily have admonished him with, "Mark, I will **not** read this paper. It is unacceptable. If this handwriting doesn't improve, you'll probably stay in third grade until you're thirty years old!"

Instead, this is what she said as she and her group of beaming third-graders greeted me for a creative writing residency: "Mimi, these are the most wonderful third grade writers! So creative and smart. Now, Mark sometimes has to have his paper translated from the original, but when he does, we read it and just love his ideas!" The whole class smiled, including Mark, who nodded his head in agreement with his teacher's description.

In a high school library, a tough-looking teen slouched through the aisles looking for a book. He kept repeating, "Where the h— is that f— book?"

The librarian could easily have sent him to the principal for his obscenity and disgraceful library behavior. But, instead, she voted for Life and sweetly said, "Have you tried looking under the F's?"

The boy immediately apologized, straightened up, and gratefully became her new best friend!

At a large performing arts center, I stood in the lobby and watched as buses from around the state unloaded schoolchildren who had come to watch a special performance of *Peter Pan*. Most of the children bounced excitedly into the auditorium, led by cheerful teachers and chaperones. Except for one group.

That morning, their teacher must have voted Death. Her face set in grim lines, she was clearly unhappy and unexcited. The children walked in strict formation, looking straight ahead with expressionless eyes, and contrasted greatly with the overwhelming number of energized dancing lines of children.

The sad little group sat in a row near me. I watched them as much as I watched the performance. Their teacher hardly looked at the stage. Glaring at the children throughout the play, she warned, prodded, and scolded them for minor crimes like not sitting up straight, crossing legs, whispering, leaning. When Tinker Bell begged the children to clap if they believed in fairies, the entire audience, except for one class, clapped joyfully. That class never moved!

Would you want your favorite child, or children, to live in such a grim class for one year? one month? one day? Everything was a BIG THING to that teacher—worth scolding, threatening, and punishing.

Gathering memories and experiences, observations and lessons from my years, I want to share a few words of wisdom that I hope will encourage you to vote Life every day.

Long ago I lived in Hawaii. The children had a popular expression that I heard daily: "Ain't no beeg theeng." When they saw someone overreact, make a mountain out of a molehill, they reminded that person that it "was no beeg theeng, bruddah!"

When you put them in perspective, *most* of the things that we think are major causes, situations worth fighting about, really are "no beeg theeng." We must choose our battles. Save our energy. Minimize tension. Use humor, kindness, surprise, imagination.

My mother had a retort for almost every situation in which I easily became frustrated, disappointed, or distressed. She said, "This should be the *worst* thing that ever happens to you!"

My mom's phrase is a good mantra. I should have recalled it during all those years when my daughter didn't want to eat breakfast before school. Every day, she left for high school resentful and angry at me for nudging, and I was frustrated and upset as I watched her go. One morning I found her in the kitchen eating a slice of cold pizza. Instead of voting Life and expressing relief and joy that she was eating *something,* I was disparaging. "Cold pizza? What kind of breakfast is that?" Once again, she slammed out of the house.

Why didn't I listen to my mother's words, "This should be the worst thing that ever happens to you"?

Why did I not hear the playful voices of my Hawaiian students, "Ain't no beeg theeng, Sistuh!"?

Cara survived those breakfastless high school days. I came through them with a little more perspective, a drop of wisdom. But we certainly had too many days that began with negativity.

Similar types of everyday situations and decisions demand a response from us in the classroom. If we, as educators, overreact to every act, word, hiccough, or burp by writing names on the board, giving points against a child, or doling out rewards and punishments, how will we build classroom communities of trust, safety, warmth, and cooperation? The children are watching us so closely. They watch as we pick our battles. They feel our passion and outrage when confronted with unkindness, bullying, indifference to the feelings of others. Those are the BIG THINGS! They are truly Life-and-Death challenges we must try to solve with a combination of intelligence, imagination, courage, articulation, and wisdom. Yes, and instinct.

Who are you? Look in the mirror. Do you see warmth, care, fun, encouragement, forgiveness, fairness, patience, and understanding, or do you see unsmiling, rigid disapproval? Would *you* like to be a child in your program?

The next time Jamie burps, decide whether it's a BIG THING or a small thing. (Note: If Jamie burped for attention, he will be disappointed in your minimal reaction.) You and the children are all too busy with the important stuff of education to make a big deal over a small thing like a burp. Let's pray that this is the worst thing that could ever happen to you, Jamie, and your class! Remember, it's "no beeg theeng," and your time is too valuable to spend it on something so trivial.

And please, the next time you see *Peter Pan,* encourage the children to clap for Tinker Bell!

The Elf and the Butterfly

Our settings should be places where children dream big dreams and teachers have the passion to help them pursue those dreams. Who knows what might happen?

He's almost 5 years old and starting all-day pre-K. He's a child who knows his own mind.

Guess what he wants to be when he grows up? Not an astronaut. Not a firefighter. Not a police officer. Not a zookeeper. You probably won't guess, so I'll tell you: He wants to be an elf! Having thought a long time about this serious decision, he can tell you all about his reasons: Elves are really good helpers. They help Santa with toys. Elves work hard and work together nicely. They have good ideas and have fun.

He hopes when he starts pre-K, he'll find lots of books about elves and even get to build an elf city as a project. (One of his friends told him they do projects in pre-K.) Once, at home, he built an elf city with Styrofoam boxes and blocks and fast-food containers, but his little sister knocked it down. (It was an accident.) Maybe his projects will be safer if he gets to build them and play with them in school. Maybe they can stay in the block area for days. He's not sure what his elf name might be, but he likes to think about it. When his teacher asks the children what they want to be when they grow up, he will proudly say, Elf!

His little sister just turned 3 years old and is entering a preschool program. Why is she so excited? Because her mom told her that she would be in the Butterfly Room! She loves butterflies—their colors are so beautiful. Her favorite butterfly colors are blue and orange, but when she draws pictures of butterflies she uses all the colors in her markers box. Even for the flowers. And clouds. If the teacher asks her what she is drawing, she'll try to explain. But sometimes grown-ups don't understand her artwork, even though she knows all about it.

She imagines the Butterfly Room filled with beautiful butterflies every day. She wants to make butterflies out of colored paper to bring on her first day. Her mom helps her cut out the wings. Once one of her friends let her wear her Halloween butterfly costume. She flew through all the rooms in the house playing butterfly with her stuffed animals. They thought she was magical—like butterflies. She can hardly wait for the exciting surprises she'll discover in the Butterfly Room.

The pre-K teacher knows that it is important to create a classroom environment that reflects the individual characteristics of each child. She checks the children's names and the information that was provided by families and included in their individual portfolios from previous teachers. She wants to know who has allergies. Who's a thumb sucker? Who can write his name? Who is a talker? Who is shy? She scrambles to get ready for all the children.

Even though the teacher has been teaching for over 25 years, every new class is a new experience. This concept has been hard to convey to her many student teachers over the years, but she is sure they will find out for themselves.

Displays of brightly colored books related to the children's interests—volcanoes, polar bears, and firefighters—fill the tables and shelves. Posters and photos of children representing many different cultures adorn the walls. Charts with space for children's names, photos, and ideas wait for new artists.

She is still learning about the special interests of every child. She is vexed because that information is always high on her priority list; she sends home a friendly welcome and questionnaire to families before school begins. She has a perfect record for connecting the children's interests with her curriculum because she knows that when people make meaningful connections to their own fascinations, the learning that happens is deeper and more relevant. Engaged children are more likely to feel comfortable in the classroom and ready to learn how to get along with each other.

Some of her colleagues chide her and warn that with all the benchmarks, guidelines, and directives coming down from local, state, and national agencies, there will be little time for her celebration of children's special interests. A veteran, passionately dedicated teacher, she'll find ways to honor the favorite topics of every child. She always has!

She has no idea that one of her students aspires to be an elf. But she has no doubt that in her class, even an elf will have rich, relevant, and joyful experiences!

Reassigned from the Bunny Room, the Butterfly Room teacher is searching for butterfly treasures for the young children soon to begin their new school year. She tries hard to give life to her room's theme rather than limit its importance to the label and a poster or two. When she was in the Bunny Room, she collected an array of poems, stories, pictures, books, and games celebrating bunnies—and now she is doing the same for butterflies. She knows that not every child will be fascinated by butterflies, but they will all feel a sense of identity and community knowing that they are part of the Butterfly Room.

She is already thinking of creative movement ideas to represent the amazing, magical transformation of caterpillars to butterflies. She imagines this story playing out over days—the caterpillar time, the cocoon time, then the time of change and flying out with all-new, gorgeous colors. There are so many musical possibilities to accompany each component of this drama. Children will learn some science, music, movement, and language skills along with the opportunities to express their creativity and expend some energy.

Even if the children are indifferent to butterflies now, she is sure that after this year in the Butterfly Room, they will all find butterflies interesting. Maybe even one or two of the children will already have a special interest in butterflies. She can't wait to find out.

A future elf gathers boxes and fast-food containers for his first project in pre-K. He just knows pre-K will be the *best* time ever! He can't wait to meet his teacher. Maybe there will be another child in his room who dreams of being an elf.

The little butterfly girl saves the sheets of pink and yellow tissue paper that came in a package for her mom. Pink and yellow butterfly wings are so beautiful. She assures her stuffed animals that she will tell them everything— *everything*—about the Butterfly Room after her first day in preschool. There will be so much to tell!

Once Upon a Time
The End!

As children are welcomed by us (and we by them) into the enchantment of stories, they become more skilled at storytelling, their academic skills are strengthened, and their too-often diminishing spirits are nourished.

What do we want our children to learn? I'm sure our wish list would include such noble goals as language development, comprehension, vocabulary recognition, listening skills, communication and cooperative learning skills, respect, multicultural understanding, verbal skills, imagination, creativity, literature appreciation, self-confidence, and self-esteem.

These important proficiencies are acquired through myriad methodologies and materials. In our too-often test-driven time, with schedules growing tighter by the moment to make room for practicing for tests, for scoring and measuring, we may easily forget a time-tested, universally delightful, and beloved way of learning—stories! Stories fit all ages, places, time frames, and circumstances. They can happen on a walk, in a car, in the water, in an airport, on a visit. They can even happen in a gym or in a classroom or outdoors. As we fall under the magical spell of stories, we check off items on our learning wish list. Those excellent outcomes are woven into the colorful patterns we continually create in the telling, the listening to, the celebration of stories.

Chloe, who has just turned 3, runs to greet us at the airport. As we wait to claim our bags, she puts in her request: "Tell me a story!"

"Shall we use your name?"

At 3, we want our names to be at the center of all our stories.

"Yes. Tell it about Chloe."

"What do you want our story to be about?"

Chloe is into animals, dinosaurs, lost and found, and mean and nice. I'm not surprised when she says, "A turtle."

"Once upon a time there was a very shy little turtle who always hid in her shell." We crunch down, into our shells. Chloe hides her face. "I'm in my shell," she whispers from behind her hiding hands.

"Everyone was looking for the little turtle but couldn't find her. All they could see was a green turtle shell."

While Chloe's mom and dad pick up the luggage, the little turtle stays hidden in her shell, waiting for a friendly person to find her.

"Finally, along came a very nice girl named—what do you think?"

"Chloe!"

"Right! Chloe came skipping along." The turtle emerges from her shell and turns into a skipping Chloe.

"Chloe sees the shy little turtle shell and says, 'C'mon out, little turtle. Don't be afraid. I won't hurt you. You can come home and live with us!'"

Chloe peeks from behind her hands. A shy smile warms her turtle face.

"And they lived happily ever after."

Before Chloe stops clapping for that story, she is already requesting another. And another and another. We tell stories about the mean dragon who turned nice and the mean girl who turned nice, but mostly about the shy turtle who found a friend named Chloe.

Finally, I suggest, "It's your turn, honey. How about telling Grandma Mimi a story?"

In her most dramatic storytelling voice, she says: "Once upon a time. The end!"

Ryan (2) must have a horse in every story. Big sister Callie (5) loves stories about friends, family, activities, animals, fairies, princesses, elves.

As we burst into the house for our visit, we are greeted by two children chanting, "A story! A story!"

We sit on the floor and tell our stories. Ryan decides on the color of his horse: black.

We clap a galloping rhythm, slap our thighs, thump the floor, "Giddyap! Giddyap!"

"Once upon a time, this beautiful horse was galloping through the woods."

"The enchanted woods," corrects Callie.

"Of course, the enchanted woods. The horse is singing a beautiful horse song. Can you sing it?"

"I'm a beautiful horse, ho, ho, ho, a beautiful horse, ho, ho, ho," Callie sings.

"Ho, ho, ho," joins in Ryan, so happy to have a story that begins with a horse.

"The horse could be looking for a princess to ride him," Callie suggests.

"Great idea! The beautiful horse had no princess to ride him. He looked everywhere for a princess and finally . . ."

"He found her sleeping in the forest."

Callie and I go on with the story, with sparks of "ho, ho" from Ryan, along with galloping handclaps to accompany the search.

When the horse finally finds the sleeping princess, she wakes up and jumps on him and they gallop away together. Callie jumps up, runs to her crayons and markers, and announces, "We better do some pictures about this story—Ryan, want to make a horse?"

"Stories need pictures!" Callie proclaims as she begins her illustrations.

Five-year-old Marissa loves the stories her grandmother, Sarah (whom Marissa calls Bimi), tells her. One day they were riding along discussing a recent news story about a car that fell into a hole. Oh, it was a big discussion! They wondered how it would feel to fall into a hole. Suddenly, Marissa turned to her grandmother and said, "I want to tell you a story, Bimi."

Sarah was thrilled. Marissa started her story.

"Well, there was this little girl who fell into a hole that went into another hole that went into a cave. She found a red flower and picked it. She came back with the flower. Everyone wanted it. She gave it away. So she went back to the cave to get another flower and she couldn't get in. So everyone had to figure out how to grow their own flowers."

Sarah exclaimed, "Oh, Marissa. It's so nice to have you tell me a story!"

"Bimi, does that remind you of when you were a little girl and someone told you a story?"

"It sure does—where did you get that story?"

"I believe everything with my imagination!" Marissa said.

Treading water for half an hour while my skin puckers and my toes begin to grow webbing, I eavesdrop on five children playing Little Mermaid on the other side of the pool. They talk nonstop about who's playing what character, what each one says, what comes next in the story.

"I'm Ariel and you be Ursula."

"I don't want to be Ursula."

"You can't sing when your tongue is cut out, no more."

"I want to be Ariel's father."

I am mesmerized as I listen and watch the children splash, jump, dive, dialogue, sing, and argue the story. This is the third day they have played Little Mermaid in the pool. They saw the video three days ago.

They are still deep into the story when their mother calls them out for dinner.

"But I can't walk yet. I have no legs," the Little Mermaid protests.

"I'll carry you, Ariel," the mom says, and wraps the Little Mermaid in a tie-dye beach towel.

The third-graders are prancing, jogging, leaping, and skipping around the gym, warming up for our story.

"Once upon a time," I begin, "this kid was out in the beautiful woods on a gorgeous day like today. So much energy! What could that kid be doing?"

Ideas always come fast and furiously.

"Running."

"Skipping."

"Bouncing a ball."

"Dancing."

We choreograph all the suggestions and arrange them in a sequence. Today I play rhythmical percussion music from the Middle East as the children run, jump rope, skip, pick flowers, dance, and bounce balls in creative movement around the gym.

I always ask the students to make choices, so I shout, "Everyone choose your favorite part and dance it!"

Twenty-six different ideas and patterns. We change to another favorite and celebrate it. What a beautiful day in the woods!

We rest. We catch our breath. I continue with the story.

"Well, after so much energetic activity, that kid was exhausted. Whew! And hungry, too. But, there is no-fast food restaurant or picnic table in sight. Nothing to eat and nowhere to rest, but—wait, what's that across the field in the woods? A little house."

I tap a knocking rhythm on my tambourine. "Let's knock on the door. No one home. Let's try again."

Tap. Tap. Tap.

"Let's turn the doorknob to see if anyone is home."

We all twist our wrists and hands to find. . . .

"Uh-oh! No one is home, but the door is open! Shall we go inside?"

We walk together to a steady tambourine beat. "There, on a table, the kid sees three bowls of porridge—a big bowl, a medium-sized bowl, and a little bowl."

The story is interrupted by a third-grader who bursts with the discovery: "It's Goldilocks!"

And so it is. Laughing, dancing, chanting, we go on with the story. Surprise!

Folktales from around the world are the focus of the fifth-graders. Today, we will play with the story of Ananci and the story box. Through music, drama, dance, and dialogue, followed by visual arts and creative writing, we freely adapt the story. The marvelous African rhythms of Montego Joe accompany our dance-drama as everyone dances all the characters, all the actions of the story.

We dance the proud, powerful Sky God and the spider, Ananci, spinning a web from Earth to sky, then climbing up till he reaches the Sky God.

We dance the Sky God presenting his treasured story box, which contains all the stories in the world. We show how Ananci wants the story box, but the Sky God demands that he meet three challenges first:

"Bring me the leopard with the gleaming teeth, the stinging hornets, and the impossible-to-see little spirit ghost."

We dance Ananci climbing back to Earth down his ladder web and searching for the leopard, the hornets, and the spirit ghost. As he catches each one of them, he dances with joy. Now up, up, up the ladder they climb, back to the Sky God. Yes, here they are!

The leopard pounces across the sky. The buzzing hornets buzz. The elusive little spirit ghost sways and swirls, never keeping the same shape.

Ananci is presented with the story box and cannot wait to open it. He lifts the cover and all—all—the stories of the world float down to earth, every single one of them, and they are floating still to this very day.

"Oops," I say. "I think a story just landed on your shoulder. Did you just step on a story? Look in your pocket, you might find a story hiding there!"

The fifth-graders walk home looking for stories, waiting for stories to find them, to land on them, to float down to them as they keep on the lookout.

The next day, every child comes to school with a story to tell, to write, to illustrate, to dance, to read, to sing, to recite, to sculpt, to share.

Children celebrate stories in different ways:

"Stories need pictures!" says Callie.

"Ho, ho, ho," says Ryan.

"It's Goldilocks!" says Scott.

"I believe everything with my imagination!" says Marissa.

"Once upon a time. The end," says Chloe.

What do *you* say? How do you celebrate stories?

Whether we follow these stories while treading water or driving through holiday traffic, we can imagine the fascination, the excitement of the children in the experience of storytelling. Storytelling (unless it's reduced to a test question on a standardized exam) is a dynamic and creative process. Stories are told and retold, changed and rearranged. Vocabularies grow. Understanding of plot, character, conflict, and drama increases. The abilities to make comparisons, see relationships, and find connections expand. Are our stories true or made-up? Are they fiction or nonfiction? Can we predict their endings? Do they include chants, poems, refrains? Are they rhythmic? Are they full of mysteries? Stories as old as caves and as new as today all celebrate language, enriching imagination and wonder—our uniquely human gifts.

When we make room in our rooms, when we make time in our time for the sharing of stories, we help children learn about the story in history, the adventures of journeys, the overcoming of obstacles, and the miracles of courage, faith, and wit.

"Do Spiderwebs Ever Wake You Up?" Oh, the Wonder of It All!

Young children keep us from getting stuck in neutral. They make us take back roads, stop for scenic views. When we hang out with them, we are always connected to amazement. They surprise us!

It always tickles me when folks ask, "Are you still hanging out with little kids?" As if there's some cosmic cutoff time to get on with one's life and commit to a more serious profession! I've long passed that cutoff date. I usually respond with something like this: "Am I still hanging out with little kids? Is the sky still up? Is water still wet? Of course, darling, till my last breath!"

People who do not walk around with their sweater sleeves pulled out of shape by small, paint-stained, sweaty hands; who do not have smudge marks on their faces from kisses pressed by tiny lips smeared with colored markers; who do not cut up their companions' food into bite-sized portions at gala dinner parties; who do not go on trips and shout, "Look, everyone! Cows! How many cows do you see?"; whose efficiently structured daily lives are filled with mature conversations and activities often wonder *why* I hang out with young children.

Sometimes I give them an answer like, "Because they're there." Sometimes I shrug and say, "Just lucky, I guess." Sometimes I laugh. "Darned if I know," I say.

But I really do know. I hang out with children because *I have to!*

In this fast-lane, topsy-turvy, high-tech whirl of a world, where cool is hot and yes is not, where violence is epidemic and the lessons of history are seldom learned, being with young children is like aerobics for the imagination, nourishment for the spirit. Sharing time with young children is like a splash in a deliciously cold, energizing lake on a smoggy, muggy day. Children tell you things like, "My birthday is coming to my house next week!" (Cheyenne). They ask questions like, "Daddy, do you remember when you first saw me?" (Noah). They respond to instructions to pick up their rooms with, "Mommy, I'm not the person for this!" (Domenico). They pay a mourning call on a grieving neighbor by consoling him with "Is your dog still dead?" (Tonya).

The honesty of young children is startling. My 6-year-old friend Maria looked at my naked face with her clear eyes and asked, "Mimi, why are you so old?" Before I could answer, she took my hand and in a worried voice said, "I hope you don't die."

Being with children is a matter of life and death! It takes courage to spend time with young children. It takes a tough skin and a mushy heart. Young children keep me honest and brave.

In this crazy world of stereotyped thinking, of mass media images and trite phrases, young children demonstrate originality as they share their love affair with language, with life.

When Brian announced that he had lost his first tooth, I asked him what he did with it.

"Put it under my pillow."

"What did you get?"

"I got a dollar!"

"Who gave you the dollar?" I asked.

"The Truth Fairy!"

Solving problems inventively in their expanding worlds is native to young children.

Jackie, another first-tooth loser, was excited as she told me about how her tooth fell out.

"Did you hide it under your pillow?" I asked in the familiar litany.

Jackie's voice dropped to barely a whisper. "No," she confided.

"Oh, why not, honey?"

"I didn't want the Tooth Fairy to come into my room . . ."

"So, what did you do?"

"I put my tooth on the top step of the stairs."

"Did the Tooth Fairy leave you anything?"

"Yes!" she exclaimed happily. "She left a quarter on the step!"

Young children remind us that the world is new and belongs to them. They own the moon, the sun, the stars, the songs.

Grandpa Joe was singing "Old McDonald" to his 2-year-old friend Pnina.

"No, Grandpa Joe. No!" Pnina tried to shush him.

Grandpa Joe stopped singing. Pnina wagged her finger at him.

"No, Grandpa Joe, Pnina's 'Old McDonald Had a Farm!' *My* song!"

Why do I hang out with young children? Because being with young children is a lesson in loving. In our statistical society, where feelings are hoarded, measured, metered, and splintered, we learn about wholeness.

Four-year-old Oren's mom watched in shock from the kitchen window as Oren picked every flower in the garden. He ran to the back door, presenting his treasure to her.

"These are for you, Mommy."

"Oren, one flower would have been enough for me. You didn't have to pick all the flowers!"

"No, Mommy," the little boy explained. "I love you too much for just one flower. I love you more than all the flowers!"

I spend time with young children so that I can be continually astonished. Their observations delight and inspire me. Their questions challenge me to face my own immense ignorance.

I was sitting with a few young children around a library table, talking about their favorite kinds of clothing. I was taking notes because these were interviews for the textbook I was writing.

As they shared their opinions about styles and colors, they moved closer to me. The smallest child settled in my lap. My pen scribbled along with their conversation about Sunday clothes, sandals, blue jeans, Mickey Mouse T-shirts. In the midst of the lively exchange, 5-year-old Aleah looked at me with wide eyes and asked, "Mimi, do spiderwebs ever wake you up?"

When I'm with young children, I wish on Twinkle Twinkle Little Star, I clap for Tinker Bell, I cry for the spider Charlotte, I brake for beauty, I notice a single ant climbing a blade of grass, I grow toward the light. The magical wisdom of young children is contagious.

I was explaining to a group of 3- and 4-year-olds on the last day of preschool that my little dog puppet, Snowball, was going to Peekaboo Summer Camp so he could keep practicing the peekaboo trick—he could never get it right. Some of the children smiled and said, "We're going to camp too." A few just looked and nodded. The older, more sophisticated 4-year-olds watched me with X-ray eyes.

Know-it-all Brett challenged me: "He's *really* a puppet, isn't he?"

"Yes, of course he is."

Brett pondered a few seconds, then came over and kissed the little peekaboo student. "Have a good time in camp, Snowball!"

Children comfort you with existential challenges. Some years ago, my then 95-year-old mother and I were eating lunch at a fast-food restaurant. Nearby, two children and their moms were doing the same. We ate and waved and smiled at the two 3-year-olds, who waved and smiled back at us. One of the two, Jamie, hung over the booth, peering into our eyes, and finally asked, "Are you old or new?"

Mom and I hastily bit into our sandwiches to avoid giving an immediate answer. Chewing slowly, I munched over some possible answers:

Old in years, but New in possibilities.

Old in experiences, but New in whatever is in store.

Old in yesterdays, but New in todays and tomorrows.

Old in feelings, but New in dreams.

Old in fears, but New in hopes.

Old in memories, but New in beginnings.

Old in habits, but New in breaking habits.

Old in the known, but New in the unknown.

Old in old tricks, but New in adventures.

Old in learning, but New in unlearning.

Old in being, but New in becoming.

Old in hibernating, but New in emerging.

Old in what I forgot, New in what I remember.

"What do *you* think, Jamie?" I finally said. Are we old or new?"

He bit into his chicken nugget. We knew he was contemplating the many ways he could answer our challenge. Thankfully, before he was able to share his wisdom, his mom called him to finish his fries. Whew! A close call!

Walking to the car with my mother, I thought of all the "old" teachers with years of experience in their hearts, minds, and hands. Their energy, openness, and willingness to risk and to try unfamiliar, new ideas are boundless. Their stubborn commitment to their beliefs and their promises to teach in joyful and loving ways in the midst of devastating pressures to avoid the scenic route and keep to the narrow limits of test-driven schedules and curriculum are inspiring. Yes, they may be old in years but they are very, very new in spirit. Sadly, I am also reminded of a few "new" teachers already rigid in their methods and goals, narrow in their views of children, unwilling to share and exchange materials and ideas. They may be new in years, but they are old, old, old.

Despite such traumatic encounters with the spontaneous, unpredictable, totally honest, pure curiosity of young children, I still hang out with them. (Do you?)

Why? Because in all my years, no one had ever before asked me the answer-defying question, "Do spiderwebs ever wake you up?"

(And, how are we helping our children keep the wonder?)

A Letter to the Families and Friends of the Children in Room 13

Remember those "wolves" we talked about earlier—administrators, parents, and others who sometimes question whether children are really learning from your developmentally appropriate practices? Sometimes you may need to help parents understand how your setting fosters their children's development and active engagement in learning. This letter delightfully illustrates a way to do just that.

Thank you for responding to our call for scrounge items. When you come to the open house next week, you'll notice that our huge basket of stuff is almost empty! Look for remnants of it in our homemade instruments, inventions, puzzles, museum exhibits, collections, and constructions, and in our imaginative sculpture show in the gallery area. Amazing what our talented kindergarten artists and scholars created from your cereal boxes, egg crates, coffee cans, paper towel rolls, clear plastic boxes, and Styrofoam containers. Please keep these excellent materials coming in, as we have many more things to do with them, always. The children are becoming more aware of how often we just toss away such valuable materials, so our scrounge works help our environment, too.

Thanks for answering the survey letter we sent out during the first week of school, asking you to jot down any areas of your experience that you're willing to share with the children. We've already welcomed three honored guests and learned a lot from them:

- Adam's grandfather told us about his work as a school custodian. The children listened intently as he talked about all the things he has to do to keep a school running smoothly and safely. They asked some very thoughtful questions.

- Anthony's aunt taught the children how to design and make lovely bead patterns and introduced them to braiding. This is marvelous for small and large motor skills (as well as counting, colors, and sorting).

- Destiny's mom told us about her job working in the housewares department of a big department store. The children loved the catalogs she shared and were fascinated by all the different household items and appliances she had to know about.

Of course, all of our classroom guests received beautifully written and illustrated thank-you letters from each child.

Now, about room 13, Our Place. Some of you have expressed concern that the kindergartners in room 9 down the hall seem to be more focused on practicing basic skills than our children here in room 13. You were impressed with their seatwork, paperwork, and structured lessons. We respect the different ways children are learning in our school, and we are eager to tell you about the developmentally appropriate practices approach we are sharing with your children in Our Place. We deeply believe that the students in room 13 are learning their basic skills, but in diverse ways, which we will try to describe and which you'll have the chance to see for yourselves at the open house next week (or at any time you care to visit us— you're always welcome).

You may notice that our room is a bit cluttered! So much is happening here that sometimes it's impossible to get organized and neat (even for the open house).

Our dress-up center is very popular (thanks to those of you who sent in the clothing—the children love it). Our M. N. M. trio (Monte, Nicole, and Michele) are deeply into playing with their costumes first thing every morning. It's wonderful to see all the oral language, vocabulary, listening skills, and social development that grow from their dress-up dramas!

You'll understand why we advocated for keeping our sandbox when you see how most of the children enjoy it. We think they must be the descendants of desert people! Especially Tiffany and Juan, who lead the group to the sand every free-activity time. Among their numerous projects are tunnels, cities, buried treasures (they love playing archaeologists), and sand-scapes. Last week, Latia joined in and surprised everyone by writing the whole alphabet in the sand. We called it "sandmanship." The children are learning so much about measuring—cups, pints, quarts, gallons—in their world of sand.

Be careful when you stop at the inventions lab. Lamar and Jennifer are deep at work on a very intricate invention-in-progress. We can't wait for them to introduce it and explain it to us. Remember, these scientific breakthroughs take time, so we have to be patient. A lot of problem solving, decision making, and cooperative learning go along with this invention. They promised to try to finish it in time for our science fair (which you will learn about soon).

Have the children told you about their fabulous musical instruments? They're constructed of and decorated with scrounge and found objects, in colorful and original ways. Every day we use our instruments for stories, parades, sound effects, math, science, special events. In our weather study, we composed a blustery thunderstorm symphony. On Tuesday, we enriched our math lesson by adding one instrument at a time until we listened to the sum of all the parts. Then we subtracted one after another until we had silence—zero. We like to compose rhythms using numbers and patterns. Of course, we can't help dancing to our wonderful music! You would too! (We often write down our choreography. For example, 10 jumps/5 kicks/10 jumping claps/2 wiggle-wiggles/repeat.) Easy to follow and so much fun to do. If we have time, we'll demonstrate at the open house.

Our room is drenched in language! Words! Posters! Signs! Charts! Cartoon labels! Letters! Our word wall is packed with words the children suggest and recognize. Doesn't it make great wallpaper? The class rules prominently posted on the door were discussed and agreed upon by the children. Our mailbox is bursting with mail, which gets delivered every day. It takes time to help the children write and read their letters. They love to get mail! Notice the postage stamps they designed. Their letter and word recognition and comprehension are strengthened every day in everything we do.

The orange flip chart near the nature table is our songbook. Look through its large, bright pages. Read the words to all the songs your children know. The music teacher is on maternity leave, but we sing every day anyway. The children recognize every song and follow the words as we sing. Is this singing or reading? (We say it's both!) We love the illustrations the children designed for each song.

Reading is happening all the time in Our Place. We don't limit reading to one specific time slot. We're almost finished with the Ananci stories. We read a story or a poem every day after lunch. Our nature-loving students are immersed in books about butterflies, dinosaurs, fish, and volcanoes. All the children are fascinated by the variations of the Cinderella story told by people around the world. Even though the holidays are still far off, the children want to hear Michael J. Rosen's *Elijah's Angel* over and over!

And our children count! Numbers are everywhere in Our Place. We count days, months, colors, shoes, pockets, loose teeth, pebbles, clouds. We measure and graph everything. Right now, our birthday graph is very popular.

We mustn't forget to tell you about the turtle. One of our colleagues from a nearby school was driving along when she saw a huge turtle in the middle of the road. Thrilled to find such a serendipitous treasure, and thinking of how her second-graders would love to meet such an interesting animal, she jumped out of her car to pick it up. As she carefully set it in the backseat, she remembered that her school was committed to a very rigid, tightly scheduled, solidly structured curriculum with very little time for any diversion. Most of each day was spent preparing the children for testing, practicing skills and drills in a school-wide teaching program. Reluctantly, she gave the turtle to us.

We can't begin to describe the countless ways our turtle has inspired rich and meaningful learning experiences! Check out the shelf of books about turtles that the children are reading. Their questions about turtles filled our wonder chart and started us off on research and adventures. You'll learn from their turtle books and charts about different kinds of turtles—like snapping turtles, painted turtles, box turtles. In the turtle log, next to the habitat the children built, they've written very interesting observations. You'll see how their handwriting is growing clearer every day. Their vocabulary continually delights us. We've discovered many turtle legends and myths from different cultures. At the beginning of the year, we didn't know that the turtle is a very important animal and symbol in many traditions! Did you? Next week, at the open house, the children will present their own interpretation of the legend of Turtle Island, accompanied by original music, dialogue, chants, and dances. The costumes, props, and scenery were built from your scrounge materials. Soon you'll receive your invitation to the program made for you by your kindergartner.

Our newest classmate, Molly, who came from China last month, is learning more and more English each day. All of her class neighbors are excellent tutors and we do so much talking all the time. (How else to learn a language but to talk a lot?) Yesterday, on our field trip to a nearby field, all the children wanted to hold Molly's hand and be her helpers as we celebrated our senses and wrote and drew impressions of our field study in our sketchbooks.

When you come to the open house, you'll see our classroom helpers board, with jobs for every child every day. Many of the 24 jobs were suggested by the children. It takes all of us working together to contribute to the success and happiness of our group.

Included in your open house packet next week will be a description of developmentally appropriate practices from the National Association for the Education of Young Children, as well as an informational sheet about the multiple intelligences. (We all learn through and from our own unique mix of strengths and interests.)

We're eager to welcome you and tell you how much we love your children and how happy we are to be with them in Our Place, room 13.

Sincerely,
The Teachers of the Children in Room 13

P.S. We've had a few instances when children were *really* sick (fever, etc.) but tried to hide their symptoms so they could come to school. The third grade brother of one of our students explained that his sister was "playing healthy" so she wouldn't miss school. We are flattered, but naturally we are concerned about all our children's well-being. Thank you.

Acknowledgments

Joseph Bruchac titled his gathering of Native American Poems and Songs, *The Circle of Thanks*. I love that title and wish, in my unbelievable ever expanding circle, I could thank everyone I ever met in the world! The names of each and all the friends, neighbors, students, families, children walking along the way together, lovingly sharing, would fill library shelves!

Because we are always caught in time and space, let me thank as many of the dear people in my circle of thanks as limitations allow. Since 1970, I have been the luckiest person to share movement, stories, and music with ALL the children in the Early Childhood Program of the Leo Yassenoff Jewish Center in Columbus, decades of fantastic kids and teachers. Thank you, Carol Folkerth, director of the JC, and Taryn Terwilliger, Nikki Henry, Leslie Rosen, and all our beautiful staff for all these years of joy.

Since its inception, decades ago, Columbus's Artists-in-Schools program has brought and brings artists in all fields into classrooms that enrich our children's lives. A-I-S is now part of Donna Collins's vitally important organization, Ohio Alliance for Arts Education. Tim Katz and Oulanje Regan coordinate and inspire this outstanding program and help me burst into countless classrooms with gifts of fun and creativity.

Bobbie Grawemeyer, Christie Creagh, Stacey Raymond, and staff of the Early Childhood Department of Columbus State Community College have set out a warm welcome mat to my course, Playing with the Arts, that is ongoing and awesome. Thanks, Columbus State Community College.

Niki Fayne first invited me to teach at Otterbein University decades ago! My course, Arts Across the Curriculum, is still thriving! Thanks, Claire Parsons, Sue Constable. and Otterbein staff, for your constant support and love.

The Columbus Metropolitan Libraries have been honored as one of the outstanding library systems in the country. Patrick Losinski, our director, offers many innovative programs. Our libraries' annual summer programs are greeted by thousands of children of all ages who are treated to hours of delight in all arts areas. Karen Bell and her staff coordinate the summer presentations. I have been so lucky to be part of so many children's summers in the libraries with my "Hangin' Out With the 'Queen of Fun'" sessions.

Since 1970, I have been the "mother" of OSU Hillel Foundation's Folk Dance program. My dance gang has sustained my spirit through all seasons and reasons! Cicily Sweet, Adit, and Neev Granite have helped lead and teach. Each and all of our truly fabulous dancers have contributed to the warmth and joy. Children of all ages have always been welcomed to our dance circles. Joseph Kahane, director of OSU Hillel Foundation, and his wonderful staff have kept Hillel's doors wide open to our group, Columbus's first and oldest center of folk dancing in the city.

More than 30 years ago, I was one of the founders of Days of Creation–Arts For Kids, an innovative, arts-rich program that has reached thousands of children throughout central Ohio. Aaron Leventhal, Kaye and Phil Boiarski, Allen and Leslie Zak, and Larry Hamill were my cohorts in that terrific and very successful venture that inspired many other programs for children to include the arts as one of their basic offerings. Hugs to all our outstanding artists/teachers who enriched the program over the years.

Ohio Association for Education of Young Children (OAEYC) is one of our nation's best state affiliates! For years and years, they have made room for me to share and celebrate with teachers from across the state! Thanks dear Kim Tice, Beri Tiffany-Smith, Sherry Roush, Lisa Mandelert, and all you wonderful OAEYC members and helpers.

Angie May-Brewer, Lea Ann Hall, and the wonderful leaders and helpers of the Columbus Association for Education of Young Children have been and are my partners in good causes!

Fred Andrle and Ann Fisher, stellar hosts on WOSU FM (NPR) call-in programs, welcomed and still welcome me to share my very opinionated and passionately charged beliefs about children, the arts, play, and the possibility of joy in learning on their radio programs through the years. I am very grateful for those opportunities.

Jane Hawes, editor of *Columbus Parent,* invited me to be a regular contributor to her excellent newspaper. See above for the themes I am able to write about through the year. I am very grateful to you, Jane.

Teachers, families, friends, and all those along this incredible journey who have walked, talked, laughed, cried, and danced with me along the way, including Sarni Dickerson, Ronni Richards, Maureen Reedy, Marlene Robbins, Judy Phohl, Yael Steinfeld, Michael Joel Rosen (poster child for creativity), Cathy Arment, Dawn Heyman, Tom Tenerovitch, Janis Pechenik, Tom Griffen, Debbie (Rainbow Girl) Clement, Ira "Twangs," Rose Stough, Tom Griffin, Lorraine Arcus, Hillary Fink, Debbie Charna, Kathy Harris, Connie Dow, Enrique Feldman, Candace Mazur, Karen Crockett, Sylvia Jackson, Yael Steinfeld . . . My list of special people who have made such a difference in my life is endless. I wish I could name each and all of you. You are written in my heart.

Thanks, Stevie Wonder, for the "key of life."

To my sister, Laura Walcher, loving, tough editor; my bro, Mike Kaplan, drums his love; my sister in love, Marilyn Cohen, teacher extraordinaire; my niece, Caryn Falvey, awesome principal; Bob Walcher and Herb Cohen, my bros in love; and to the family tribes—Cohens, Blooms, Walchers, O'Briens, Falveys, Wilbats, Gandals, Jacobsons, Newmans, Falveys, Rappoports, Selingers, and Kaplans—thank you each and all in my most inner circle of love and support.

Polly Greenberg, former editor of *Young Children,* educator, and author, special hugs and thanks from the heart for opening the doors of NAEYC's *Young Children* to my early writings. Carol Copple and Millie Riley edited and helped birth the first edition of *Teaching in the Key of Life.* I am indebted to Kathy Charner, Derry Koralek, Holly Bohart, Liz Wegner, Malini Dominey, and Eddie Malstrom for their unbelievable caring and energy to make this special book happen, with help from David Heath and Kyra Ostendorf at Redleaf Press.

Thank you, NAEYC and Redleaf Press, for helping me spread a lifetime of love to our precious teachers, families, and children. Even though we are all scattered around the country and the world, we are walking together on the same path, singing and full of hope.

About the Author

Born and raised in New York City, Mimi Brodsky Chenfeld began her teaching career in Albany, New York, in 1956, teaching fourth grade. Since that time, she has taught adults and children of all ages and grades, from Head Start to Upward Bound, from New York to Hawaii. Her special love is celebrating the arts and creativity in ALL her programs. Since 1970, Mimi has been totally immersed in the education and arts community in Columbus, Ohio, now her home base from which she travels extensively to be with teachers, university students, and children. The author of many poems, stories, and novels, her books *Teaching by Heart*, *Celebrating Young Children and Their Teachers*, and *Creative Experiences for Young Children* are widely used. Her children's novel, *The House at 12 Rose Street*, one of the first controversial stories for children, was adapted for an After School Special and nominated for an Emmy.

The recipient of many honors, Mimi's favorite comes from a child who wrote, "Mimi, you are the Queen of Fun!"